SELECTED POEMS
1910–1960

Novels

SCISSORS
SAILS OF SUNSET
THE LOVE RACK
LITTLE MRS MANINGTON
SAGUSTO
DAVID AND DIANA
INDIANA JANE
PAMELA'S SPRING SONG
HAVANA BOUND
SPEARS AGAINST US
PILGRIM COTTAGE
THE GUESTS ARRIVE
VOLCANO
VICTORIA FOUR-THIRTY
THEY WANTED TO LIVE
ONE SMALL CANDLE
SO IMMORTAL A FLOWER
EIGHT FOR ETERNITY
A TERRACE IN THE SUN
THE REMARKABLE YOUNG MAN
LOVE IS LIKE THAT
THE PILGRIM COTTAGE OMNIBUS

Miscellaneous

THE DIARY OF RUSSELL BERESFORD
HALF WAY; AN AUTOBIOGRAPHY
GONE RUSTIC
GONE RAMBLING
GONE AFIELD
GONE SUNWARDS
AND SO TO BATH
AND SO TO AMERICA
AND SO TO ROME
ONE YEAR OF LIFE
PORTAL TO PARADISE

CECIL ROBERTS

Selected Poems

1910 – 1960

Preface by
LORD BIRKETT

HUTCHINSON OF LONDON

HUTCHINSON & CO. (*Publishers*) LTD
178–202 Great Portland Street, London, W.1

London Melbourne Sydney
Auckland Bombay Toronto
Johannesburg New York

★

First published 1960

821.9
British poetry

*This book has been set in Bembo type face. It has
been printed in Great Britain by The Anchor Press,
Ltd., in Tiptree, Essex, on Smooth Wove paper and
bound by Taylor Garnett Evans & Co., Ltd., in
Watford, Herts*

The author wishes to thank the editors of the *Sunday Times*, the *Observer*, the *Cornhill*, the *English Review*, *To-Day*, the *New York Times*, *Ladies Home Journal*, and *Red Magazine*, in whose papers some of these poems appeared, and also Messrs Hodder & Stoughton Ltd for prefatory poems from *Gone Rustic*, *Gone Rambling*, *Gone Afield*.

Contents

Inscriptions

Miscellaneous

For titles marked * there is a note at the end of the volume.

Preface

I T IS a great pleasure for me to write a short prefatory word to this volume of *Selected Poems* written by my friend Cecil Roberts. He is known throughout the English-speaking world, and much farther afield, as a novelist and essayist of great distinction. His work has won for him a very secure place in the hearts of a great and admiring public. Some of his books—and I would select *Portal to Paradise* as an example—combine all the qualities of superb descriptive writing with wide historical research and profound human interest, so that they are already assured of a permanent place in our literature.

It is quite obvious that he needs no introduction or commendation from me, or from anybody else, when he ventures into another field, and presents this selection of the poems he has made during the last fifty years. But, as Bacon said, 'all these things are graceful in a friend's mouth that are blushing in a man's own', and I am glad to be given the opportunity to say so.

It was natural that from time to time, as he pursued his main tasks in life, he should turn aside to record some of the more notable experiences in poetry; notable experiences, not always because the deeper emotions were stirred, but because some slight thing, some passing thought, some fancy, some sudden memory, somehow demanded expression.

Two such poems are, I think, *The Priest of Sant' Ambrogio*, with its charming reminiscence of Max Beerbohm, and *The Old Brown Hat*, with its affectionate reference to John Betjeman. For Cecil Roberts has the poet's eye, the imagination and the insight to preserve the significant thing whether it be slight or momentous, and he possesses too the skill to set down the significant experience in choice words that give pleasure to the reader. He has a gift for friendship. He has known men and women in many lands and places, and the poems record a life full of rich human relationships that others will be glad to be allowed to share. And all through the book there runs the love of the old familiar things that are the very stuff of poetry when perceived by the inward eye. *Springtime in Cookham Dean* would appear to have been written forty years ago, but it captures the authentic note of Spring with all its scents and sounds and colours, as the poet has rejoiced to do through many centuries.

Cecil Roberts has won the praise of many poets for some of these poems; but I fancy that his deepest pleasure will be to find that this volume of poems, nourished by him through half a century, has given pleasure also to all those who care for lovely things.

I wish for this happy outcome, so that he may know something of the pleasure he has for so long given to others.

Birkett,

Invocation

Come now, my Muse, who once to Horace of old
Gave more than his Maecenas of bright gold
When, from a mint whose impress never wears,
He struck a wealth untarnished down the years;
Give me a credit in the bank of Time
That I may shower with a thriftless rhyme
Largesse more prodigal than galleons from the West
Poured in Europa's lap, or from the Quest
Jason, returning with the fabled Fleece,
Scattered, improvident, through the isles of Greece;
For I would buy one jewel from Time's store
To adorn a moment with immortal lore.

*The Moon a lovely maiden is

The moon a lovely maiden is
Who hides from me through all the day,
Enwrapped in cloudy mysteries
That fall away
At even, when she kneels to pray,
The moon a lovely maiden is.

The moon has sorrowful large eyes
And her round face is pale with fright,
What is the fear from which she flies
With face so white?
Her absence darkens the dark night,
The moon has sorrowful large eyes.

A maiden who has never smiled
The shy moon is, most beautiful,
Most virtuous and undefiled
And dutiful—
Yet pleasanter to kiss a skull,
A maiden who has never smiled.

Perhaps the moon no maiden is
But one who goes with silent tread
And gives a cold and solemn kiss
To all the dead,
And sleeps awhile upon each bed;
Perhaps the moon no maiden is.

Who Knows?

Who knows the world occult
Wherein there grows
The summer's rose?
What magic in the sun,
What silent toil
In secrecy begun,
What lightward thrust,
Through the dark soil
Brings beauty from the dust?

Testament

I have seen beauty beyond belief,
An English lane in summer leaf,
And walked in sleepy country towns
And felt the west wind on the downs;
Oh, I have travelled the whole world round
To find the home-place holy ground.

The Bedroom Fire

When I was a small boy
It was nice to be ill
In bed, with a fire flickering
In a room warm and still,
With long shadows walking
On ceiling and wall
And my mother's soft hands
Smoothing pillow and shawl.

And now I'm an old man
I remember, near tears,
That room with the firelight
Far off down the years,
And while the light's fading
On a life flickering out
I lie alone wondering
What it's all been about.

The room is so still
And a shadow waits there;
Oh hands that once nursed me,
Oh face once so dear,
Come closer, come closer
In the firelight's warm glow,
Ere, one journey ended,
On another I go.

The Bride

With passionless and gentle grace
The young Moon sees her bridgroom, Night,
And there is wonder in her face
Which grows the purer in his sight
Until the starry bridesmaids, crowding,
Shine more splendid in her train,
And wish her joy no moment's clouding,
No tears her radiant face to stain.

*To John Masefield

It was May, with a gleam of the sun and a rain-washed sky
When we sat in your house on the hill as we talked of the things
That drift through the mind in the hour when tea is nigh,
And your garden was noisy with chirping and flutter of wings,
All golden with blossoming broom, and full of the scent
That comes after rain; while below, falling gently away,
Ran woodlands and pastures, and there, where the sight was spent
And failed in the haze of the valley, old Oxford lay.

I do not remember the things we said in that hour,
Those were moments too pleasant to trouble our minds with their sense,
Enough were the fellowship, sight of the broom in flower—
For your plants and your beehives, the goats that came up to the fence,
Were possessions more friendly than words ever truant from truth,
Vexing the spirit that moulds them with patience, yes, more
Welcome the tangible things, when extravagant Youth
Departs with its feverish dreams after sacking Life's store.

But sometimes, in pauses, I knew you were fugitive,
And the shy gleam came to your eyes which tells me you are
A wanderer over the earth, who always will live
Drawn to the path of a dream or a wandering star;
And your voice when it bade me goodbye as the rain-clouds curled
Over the ridge of the hill, had the longing again
To sail with a fleet of dreams through the seas of the world,
To know tempests and peoples, and ports on the edge of the main.

Et in Arcadia ego

Sweet girl, whose laughter caught me under apple trees in spring,
I trod the shining ways of youth and heard my young heart sing,
For you had nineteen summers and I had twenty-one,
And I would trade the crown of years for that one jewel gone.
For is there any pearl unpriced like the shy, hurried kiss
Whose ecstasy is half a pain, and half a wordless bliss?
Oh, twice are twenty years now gone and all the paths are known,
But when a bird flutes in the trees amid the blossom blown
My heart remembers how you laughed; across the tide of years
A fallen curl, a warm red mouth, shine through a mist of tears.

*Springtime in Cookham Dean

How marvellous and fair a thing
It is to see an English Spring,
He cannot know who has not seen
The cherry trees at Cookham Dean,
Who has not seen the blossom lie
Like snowdrifts 'gainst a cloudless sky
And found the beauty of the way
Through lanes bedecked with petalled may.
It is a rare, a holy sight,
To see the hills with blossom white,
To feel the air about one flowing
With the silent rapture growing
In the hidden heart of things
That yearn, that flower, put forth wings,
And show their splendours one by one
Beneath the all-rejoicing sun.

Perhaps the joy of all the earth
Moved through us on that day of mirth
When in the morning air we trod
Hills sacred to the river god,
And heard behind us as we ran
The laughter of a hidden Pan,
Who dropped his flute because he heard
The artless cadence of a bird;
And we, who love the southern sky,
One moment ceased to wonder why
A poet in his exile cried
To see an English Spring, and sighed
Because a chaffinch on the bough
Sings and shakes the blossom now.
For who would sigh for southern skies
Who once had seen the paradise
Of this new Eden where the flowers
Drench the woods with odorous showers,

And give delight till the sense sickens
With the rapture April quickens?
This heaven where petals fall as stars,
This paradise where beauty bars
Its dew-refreshed, embowered portals
Against the clamouring of mortals,
And from green altars in dim shrines
Calls to the riven soul that pines
For leafy solitude, and prayer
That murmurs through the branches there.

When Spring in her ascension fills
The chalice of the sacred hills
With blossom like the driven snow,
And longing takes the heart, then go
On pilgrimage to Cookham Dean,
And through dim aisles of shadowed green
Dappled with the light that trembles
Round each tree, till it resembles
A maiden letting fall her hair
In cataracts of gold—draw near
The secret that brings Englishmen,
Faithful through exile, home again;
And watch the miracle of dawn,
And hear the lark, with wings upborne
Into the cloudless empyrean,
Pour his lucent, quenchless paean,
And feel the awakened senses start
In wonder at the artless art
Of orchards all in blossom showing
Against the blue of heaven glowing
Through great depths of luminous light;
Then from the windy woodland height,
Through dim ravines where tall trees wait
For day's decline to gild their state,
And touch them with caressing fingers
Of the sun-god whose smile lingers

Upon their limbs, by paths that wind
Into the valley, go—and find
The village by the water's edge
And listen to the wind-stirred sedge
That by the churchyard whispers—go
And tread the woodland paths I know,
For whosoever has not seen
The cherry trees at Cookham Dean,
Who has not roamed its hills and found
Delight in that enchanted ground,
He cannot know, he cannot tell,
Where Spring performs her miracle.

*Lines to a Dendronphobe

(For Lady Kemsley)

I was a tree, my branches raised
A green tent to the summer skies,
The bygone generations lazed
In my cool shade, a paradise
Of birds who loved, and music made
Through the long summer's cavalcade.

Stricken, in death a log I lie,
But he who felled me, Farmer Brown,
Alive, is more a log. I cry
Vengeance on this destructive clown;
Greatest of miscreants on this globe
Is Farmer Brown the Dendronphobe.

*The Elm in Leaf

I owe a grateful thought to you,
Planter unknown of this proud tree,
Some served their land at Waterloo,
Here you won immortality;
Broken the drums, the rifles rusted,
Here flourishes the lance you trusted.

The Arrow

When I caught him there
By the hawthorn bush,
With his bow drawn taught,
His mouth said 'Hush!'

'Naked boy, come down,
Let the sailor go,
He has sailed seven seas!'
But the imp said 'No!'

Ping went his arrow,
It struck. In a whirl
By the hawthorn the sailor
Took his girl.

'Look what you've done!'
I cried to young Cupid.
'The world must go on!' he grinned,
'Don't be so stupid!'

Late Marriage

Had we met thirty years ago
We had not loved in this wise way
For then, compact of fire and snow,
Life had not been a humdrum day
But one bright palimpsest of dreams,
Desires, and Time-rewarding plans,
Ere caution threw its solemn beams
Upon the scene late wisdom scans.

For thirty years ago, with joy,
What fools we would have been, and known,
Love-smitten crazy girl and boy,
Contempt for all those, wary-grown,
Who tread each step with common sense;
Poor, we had thrown a gage to Fate,
To sound advice shown insolence,
Married, and learned our wisdom late.

And now, instead of share and script,
We would have owned a brood of things,
Noisy, bright-eyed and laughter-lipped,
Music for middle-age journeyings;
For one fair girl had kept your eyes
And one tall lad had kept my strength,
And we had grown old with surprise
And not have known the journey's length.

The Roman Villa in England

How clever those Roman fingers
  Working here,
Now only a little lingers
  From that far year;
When last this pavement sounded,
  Hadrian spoke,
The trireme galleys grounded,
  From the hearth rose smoke.

How little has the landscape altered,
  These uplands green
Where Claudius' cattle faltered;
  And there between
Those fallen posts, now crumbled,
  The chariot ran,
The Roman street once rumbled
  With the traffic of man.

How futile the hopes they nourished,
  Foolish indeed,
For, even as they flourished,
  There grew Time's seed
To split their stones asunder,
  However firm,
And, ruinously, deep under,
  Worked the lowly worm.

Premonition

Dear heart, through all the afternoon
I slumbered where the woodland shade
Was deepest in the glare of June,
And as the branches o'er me swayed,
Singing that timeless song which pines
Endlessly sing as if they found
A solace in their runic lines,
I wove strange fancies to the sound;
And in each sigh I heard your sighs,
For every whisper cried—' 'Tis I!'
Until I seemed to feel your eyes
Upon me, and, I know not why,
Though you are dead, this day I felt
That union which of old we knew,
The richness of your hair I smelt
Until the wordless wonder grew
That you were here, and oh, it seemed
The years had wrought no change since last
Beneath the pine tree's shade you dreamed
With me that Future, now our Past.
Who knows, dear heart, perchance you move
Nearer in love than I in thought,
And with this premonition prove
Love is not far, and comes unsought.

When Sylvia laughs

Silver is the laughter of Sylvia,
Gold is the smile of her face,
And a pool is not bright as the eyes of her.
No fawn has an equal grace.

The poorest of those who come nigh her
Feel they are rich to behold
Such treasure as never a buyer
Bought with a crock of gold.

It's summer, the sunshine around her
Wherever she turns in her glance,
And we in good fortune, who found her,
Walk proud as the kings of Old France.

The Squire

If Squire lived well, dressed well, travelled,
  Can it be denied
Among all breeds of men
  He was England's pride?

If he ruled, rough in justice,
  Was it ever said
He took a proffered bribe,
  His honour dead?

If he lived in comfort, slept well,
  He bred brave sons
Who faced with dauntless courage
  The deadly guns.

If the Hall was his, the Living,
  The wide estate,
He knew the name of each man
  About his gate.

But these new lords who traffic
  In stock and share,
Whom else do they profit
  Playing Bull and Bear?

Ten thousand soaring shares sold
  On a rise of twenty,
To how many cottages bring they
  Food in plenty?

If Squire rode hard, swore hard, drank hard,
  Let the truth be said—
He farmed five thousand acres,
  He gave England bread.

The English Creed

Lovely the roses of old Stamboul,
And the stars in Taj Mahal's dark pool,
The cypress sentinels Garda's shore,
Wild sunsets crimson Elsinore,
    But here, together,
Roses and stars and cypress meet
    In rain-sweet weather.

An English manor house, a pond,
Green fields that slope to woods beyond,
An emerald lawn, a porch where blows
White clematis—the wanderer knows
    There's no denying
Above all other lands it's best
    To live or die in.

To a Chestnut Tree Found Stripped

Proud lady, I could weep for your distress,
   How rude of Winter to have stripped you so,
Tumbling about your feet your lovely dress,
   Leaving you naked to the winds that blow.

Poor lady, who was once all dressed in gold,
   Take heart, have you not heard the whispering?
Before the New Year's patterns all were sold
   Time placed an order with the looms of Spring.

Dear lady, you will burst with pride in May
   When you put on the new dress made for you,
A crinoline, with candle-flowers gay,
   A lovely green to match the sky's Spring blue.

Masquerade

If the faces of old houses
Bore signs of what happened within,
Some would be set in a grimace,
Some in a hearty grin,
Some would have lines still more beautiful
Than those they now show to the street,
And a Queen Anne face would entrance us
With its manner demure and sweet;
But the Georgian house might affright us
And its mask of false dignity
Fail to hide a vindictive spirit
Of the deepest malignity;
While the stark Victorian villa,
With a face of stucco and grime,
Looking murderous, is probably
Quite innocent of crime.
The Manor house, pure Tudor,
Considering the horrors within,
Should show on its face of ineffable grace
The ravages of sin;
And, strange to believe, the bungalow,
So monstrous to the sight,
If the life within took outward shape
Would fill us with delight.
Who'd think for a moment that ruinous hovel
Saw the life of Beau Brummell the Dandy,
Or that flat-faced house in the Henley Street
Was the home of the poisoner, Miss Blandy?

No, you never can tell from the face of a house
The tense drama enacted behind,
Whether love makes a heaven or lust makes a hell,
Emotions, fine, sinister, kind,
Not one leaves a trace on the outward face,

And perhaps, after all, it is well,
For what horrors we'd meet in a walk down the street,
And how difficult life might become
If the windows scowled, and the threshold throbbed,
And the walls were no longer dumb!

Lament of a lazy lover

In the heat of the day when the bees are winging
From flower to flower, and in the plain
The wheat sways not, and a low voice, singing,
Veers from the hillside and goes again,
Why do I lie so long in the sun
      With my work undone?

Folly to ask, for in idleness
Love grows apace as I watch the light,
Vine-leaf shadowed, that falls to caress
Your tresses of gold, your throat so white,
Your bodice that fits as close and thin
      As an almond skin.

When the still noon drowses with scent of flowers,
And the sheep lie down in the pine tree's shade,
When no bird sings, and the heat overpowers,
I pillow your head, and am half afraid
Lest Death might come in the guise of Sleep,
      And my dear love keep.

And yet I know, when the day, declining,
Brings cool winds to my fevered brow,
You will wake and scold me for my repining,
And, laughing lightly, demand of me how
The night shall be spent, so it's dance and song,
      And my works waits long.

*Pilgrim Cottage Poems

Cottage Dinner Party

At the oak table, in soft candlelight,
Sit my nine dinner guests, a pleasant sight:
Young Peter, with his youthful eager air,
And Ann, his sister, delicately fair.

First on my left, the serious sloe-dark eyes
Of Mrs Lane suggest my speech is wise,
While young June Trivett, wife at twenty-one,
Listens politely to the vicar's son.

First on my right, sits happy Mrs Dean,
For thirty years the County's ruling queen,
Intelligent, sweet-mannered, gay, despite
A husband who is well kept out of sight.

Lord Meaden, gourmand, holding up his glass,
Chuckles and works the jawbone of an ass,
Eyeing the brewer's widow, well content
To barter rank for unearned increment.

Brilliant, of course, as ever, Henry Hawke
Commands the table with his witty talk;
Strange that a man so gifted wastes his time
Providing friends with dinner pantomime.

Good food, good wine, I hope my table bears,
But as we eat and talk, four hundred years
Fade through the candlelight, and in the room
Ten famished serfs shiver in rush-lit gloom.

Spring Prayer

Let there be birdsong from my ancient roof,
The curl of smoke to prove a living fire,
And one dear soul within; these be the proof
God's grace has given me my heart's desire.
Blow, thou March wind, to shake the budding trees
And wake to living gold the petalled fields;
Warm is my grateful heart, with only these
I win the lasting peace contentment yields.

Town and Country

Round Piccadilly Circus the traffic roars all day,
And thousands on the pavements pursue their lonely way,
Lonelier for the thousands that still will ebb and flow
Though none comes back at all there and all forever go.

Round every Chiltern cottage a country peace is heard,
The lowing of the cattle, the song of child and bird;
No one feels ever a stranger where everyone is known
By name from birth to burial yet proudly walks alone.

Country Thoughts

When I walk by Buckingham Palace,
Where the Queen works hard all day,
Does she long to live in a cottage, I wonder,
And dream the hours away,
And never see a minister but only make decrees
Concerning new asparagus beds
And planting cherry trees?

When I walk by the Houses of Parliament
Where the grey old Thames sweeps by,
Does the Speaker forget to listen, I wonder,
And dream in his Chair, and sigh
To hear the quacking of the geese around the old barn door,
Forgetting all the garrulous flock
That fills the Commons floor?

When I walk by Hyde Park Corner,
And the trees of Rotten Row,
Guardsmen in red coats stand like tulips,
And quick the nursemaids grow,
And little tots all potted out, in prams well-bedded down,
Lift flowery faces, starry-eyed,
To brighten London Town.

When I walk by Piccadilly Circus
Where the night, in hideous rout,
Roars with a thousand wheels and turns
Like a fiery roundabout,
I close my ears to all the noise, my eyes to all the glare,
And watch a timid doe flit down
A glade by Leicester Square.

*Prayer for an old gardener

Lord God of Gardens, if you please,
Allow old Reuben Pace his ease,
The lawns are swept, the apples stored,
New beds are made, but one, O Lord,
He wishes for himself to keep
And lie there in unbroken sleep.

For sixty years he's risen early
To tend the things he's loved so dearly;
Spring, Summer, Autumn, Winter, never
Escaped an eye and hand so clever
With plants stored in the potting shed,
But now he wants to lie a-bed.

'I'm tired,' he says, 'and plants keep growing,
And proper gardeners must keep hoeing.
My back aches awful, my poor old knees
Give way beneath me.' So, Lord, please,
Allow old Reuben Pace to sleep,
Blind to the weeds that o'er him creep.

Death of an old gardener

Death came for old Reuben
At the hour of four,
He did not ring the bell
Nor tap on the door.
'Come with me, old man,
Come away,' said He,
'You had almost slipped
From my memory.'

Said old Reuben Pace
'Since you are so late
It will not harm you
A while to wait.
The 'rrhinums want bedding,
The lupins want tying,
And the lawn wants mowing—
It's no moment for dying.'

So Reuben went forth,
At the hour of eight,
To the potting shed,
But Death would not wait;
He took him suddenly,
Trowel in hand,
Ready to garden
In another land.

Ghostly Noises

Strange sounds are heard about the house at midnight,
In the hall and on the stair,
They are so furtive, and so apprehensive,
And they come upon you, unaware,
That you wonder whether they were inmates
Long ago, and one's the ghostly tread
Of the great-grandfather on the wall there,
When he took a tallow candle and went shuffling up to bed.

In the Night

How hushed the garden now the moon
  Comes round the gable of the house,
The soft enchantment grows and soon
  Will flood with light the peartree boughs.

Within the dark uncurtained room
  A blade of silver stabs the floor,
The china princess through the gloom
  Smiles on the moonstruck blackamoor.

Within his cage the budgerigar
  Opens a jet-black eye and listens,
While Nelson dies at Trafalgar
  Upon the wall; the blue jar glistens.

The French clock, made in Avignon,
  Wheezes and strikes the hour of three,
The old house settles; the night, half gone,
  Brushes the moon with a poplar tree.

Now shows the dormer window wide
  A cavern dark, with vine leaves fringed,
And in the East the refluent tide
  Of day comes back, with crimson tinged.

On Hearing Birdsong

A blackbird sang in the apple tree
And my heart leapt up for I knew beyond doubt
That the music of life would endure when we
Leave the world's last room, and to Time pass out
On the unknown way. And a thought grew strong—
Since a bird sings here, and through centuries old
Sang thus for others who passed along,
Time's not a wind so terribly cold!

The night enfolds us . . .

The night enfolds us, not a leaf is stirred,
The ringing laughter of the sunny noon
Is stilled; the busy sound of bee and bird
Comes not again, and night brings her soft boon,
For louder through the quiet now is heard
The silver weir beneath the rising moon.

Here in this garden dwell abiding things,
The green recurring pageant of the earth,
The lyric rapture of a bird that sings,
Dew on the grass, hoar frost, the simple mirth
Of little insect lives, the peace that clings
To joys exalted by their common worth.

Now in the silence comes a space for thought,
A time to think, a quiet for the mind
To brood in, and great influences, wrought
By the enduring hand of Nature, find
A healing mission in a world distraught
With all the greed and passion of mankind.

For silence is the wise man's true domain,
And Nature the great book whose wisdom leads
To tranquil days withdrawn from the world's stain
And glut of idle gossip; whoso reads
The language spoken by the wind and rain
Learns the one truth behind contending creeds.

The quest, the consummation everyone
Seeks for the thing he dreams, grows surer here,
Since little is so much, each moment spun
On looms of quietness. Peace everywhere
Settles beneath Night's wings; what we have done,
Or what remains, loses its weight of care.

After darkness

The last star pales before the dawn,
Dim is the garden as a pool
Deep in the forest; from the East
The first flush spreads, the shadows melt;
I cannot see you, O my love,
So gently breathing at my side,
But every line my fond heart knows,
Each silken curve and harmony,
Music that wakes beneath the touch.

Now after darkness, with the dawn,
The first beam comes through dormer panes,
And in the half-light, as you sigh,
You turn with drowsy-lidded smile
To the known altar of my love,
And from the chalice of your mouth
I take the morning's sacrament,
While day streams down the eastern hills,
Dews glisten and bird-music breaks.

Miss Whissitt

Will no one love Miss Whissitt?
The time is getting late,
The roses in her cheeks are wan,
The Winter will not wait;
Ten years ago, five years ago
She hoped she would not be
Left lonely on the barren bough,
A sere leaf on the tree.

Will no one love Miss Whissitt,
So gentle and so kind?
The golden tints are fading fast,
The Spring is far behind.
She smiles and still her lips are red,
And lovely are her eyes,
But no one seems to notice how
The hope within them dies.

Will no one love Miss Whissitt,
Recall a far-off day
When such a golden laughing lad
Tumbled her in the hay?
Then every bird sang merrily,
The day was at the noon,
Oh sorrow when he marched away
To drill in Death's platoon!

Will no one love Miss Whissitt,
Still winsome when she smiles,
With lovely lines about her mouth
With which she Time beguiles;
Late Summer, and the Autumn fruit
Comes crowding on the tree,
But oh, the fruit she longs to bear
And place upon her knee!

A Flight of Fancy

All day at my desk as I wrote and wrote
A thrush in the garden sang note on note,
And a vain thought came as I blotted a line—
If my words were birds, and this book of mine
Turned into a thrush's nest, these pages
Might sing their way to future ages!

Rebellion

It is good to sit in the sun and forget
The cares of life and the ills that fret
The hearts of men whose ambitious ways
Rob them of joy in these summer days.
I will sit and dream and take my rest
In this garden where summer is at its best,
Where the noonday heat brings quietness
And a lost wind touches with idle caress
The lordly tulips yellow and red;
Before me, the wooded hills are spread
Along the horizon, and faintly blue
They are part of earth and of heaven too,
And the valley's fields in various greens
Are bordered with poplars whose leafy screens
Divide the landscape like a sea
With a wave on wave of greenery.

Ah, who would talk of ambition now
When the flowery woodlands teach us how
Beauty and joy and leisured days
Are better than fortune's dizzy ways,
That he is truly wealthy who
Can sit all day with nothing to do
Save watch the old mare at the fence
Scratch her mane; or make pretence
That butterflies, in noonday hours,
Are disembodied souls of flowers
That in the evening westward fly,
Flooding with wings the crimson sky,
Staining the clouds with varied hues
That flowers for their beauty use.

The noonday murmurs with winging bees
But, more industrious than these,

The lark, with ceaseless effort, soars
To shout his song at heaven's doors
In scorn of idiot cuckoos low
On earth, who only two notes know!
And the tall poplars will not bend
Their heads nor even condescend
To throw their shadows on the ground
Where two old cows, in a profound
And tranquil meditation, keep
Aloof from woolly-headed sheep.

Nor love nor fame nor high ambition
Shall cause my heart to feel contrition
But, rebel bold, I will forget
The city's lure; nor will regret
Assail me when the evening calm
Awakens conscience, in alarm
At tasks undone, for when the Springs
Have all slipped by, and on the wings
Of old relentless Time I speed
To the oncoming Night, to plead
For one more Spring will be in vain,
The spendthrift cannot spend again;
So be it, I will lazily
Dream in the noonday heat, and be
A truant from the world, and find
The peace that fills an idle mind.

*The Village Blacksmith

In his chair in the evening, the cat on his knees,
The winter wind roaring and shaking the trees,
Sits Mark the old blacksmith, his feet on the fender,
And would not change place with a king in his splendour.

No horses come now to the smithy for shoeing,
The village is buzzing with wonders a-doing,
There's light and there's power both coming by cable,
There aren't any wonders of which they're not able!

The newspapers say there's a war in the offin',
They've unearthed an old Pharaoh, with gems in his coffin,
The Prime Minister says there's a serious crisis;
Two boys who went skating have been drowned in the Isis.

But Mark in his chair has a positive feeling
His corner is safe though the whole world is reeling;
There sits his wife sewing, God bless her dear head,
Soon she'll take a hot bottle and put in their bed.

Yes, Mark is content. When a man's eighty-five
He's settled the reason for keeping alive;
He's a wife still to love him, in the grate a live coal,
Good food in his stomach, God's peace in his soul.

*The Garden Well

At the bottom of the well,
    Fifty-eight feet deep,
Three centuries of memories
    Lie fast asleep.

If you let a stone drop,
    You break the spell,
You hear the fairies sobbing
    Deep in the well.

If you lower the bucket,
    And raise it again,
You bring up a horde
    Of hobgoblin men.

If you drink the water,
    You dream at night
Of a black-faced bride
    In a gown of white.

If you wash your face in it
    And look in the glass,
You see a young princess
    On a white horse pass.

Oh, never boil the water,
    Its steam is red,
And King Charles walks in it
    Carrying his head.

The bottom of the well,
    Fifty-eight feet deep,
Is filled with the tears
    The fairies weep.

Summer Laziness

I have not written a word today,
    The sun laughed through my apple trees,
The birds had such a lot to say,
    My poplars rustled in the breeze;
'Why write, poor fool, there's nothing in it,
Be lazy!' sang a merry linnet.

Lazy I was, and yet it seems
    I have achieved much happiness
In watching how the sunlight gleams
    Through boughs of blossoms that caress
The sky's blue face, in hearing birds
Sing to me songs that need not words.

Books we can make by taking thought,
    What sentence has a flower's grace?
What wisdom equals beauty taught
    By songbirds in a leafy place?
And all the things wise Plato knew
Provide less wonder than the dew.

All day I listened under boughs
    Where blossom fell and birds were calling;
Green waves of shadow swept my house,
    From four slim poplars, ever falling,
Soundless, through the hush of noon;
Then evening and a sickle moon.

The day slipped into dusk, the night
    Scattered a thousand stars in space,
The last wind slept, a bird in fright
    Twittered in some far woodland place;
One with the languid earth I went
To fold in sleep a day's content.

The Village Knows

The village knows Miss Whissitt,
It knows her high-laced boots,
It sees her pass with pots of flowers,
Cuttings and bulbs and roots.
'Good morning!' 'Good morning!' 'Good morning!'
She calls to the folk at their doors;
They know the enormous umbrella
She erects overhead when it pours.

The village knows Miss Whissitt,
'Disappointed in love', they say.
So a cat inherits the soft caress
A child might have known one day;
And her quick warm heart embraces
An assortment of suffering things,
Sick children, deaf grandads, lost animals,
And crazed birds with broken wings.

The village knows Miss Whissitt,
Who walks in sun or rain,
Who discusses foot-and-mouth disease
With the farmer up the lane,
Who knows the year the parson died,
And why the Squire's young son
Cannot come back to England
For something he has done.

The village knows Miss Whissitt,
It knows her smiling face,
Her stick, her hat, her keen blue eyes,
Her brooch on the bunch of lace;
They laugh, but lovingly, knowing how
This soul they deem so odd,
Through a life of countless kindnesses
Walks daily nearer God.

A Boy in the House

Who left the garden gate unlatched,
    Who left the hosepipe on the lawn,
Who used my favourite pen, who scratched
    My desk, who starts from early morn
The radio screeching, who explores
    The kitchen larder, lets the bath
Run over, rushes out of doors,
    Half-naked, down the garden path,
Indifferent to the bitter weather—
    Who sewed my trouser-legs together?

Whose shoes are these with laces knotted,
    Whose shorts are these flung anyhow,
Whose shirt is this with jam stains spotted?
    Young villain, I have caught you now!
But just too late since you are sleeping,
    Your head pressed deep in the white pillow,
Your brown throat from your jacket peeping,
    Your hair like a gold tumbling billow;
Is this the boy I must accuse
    Of putting tintacks in my shoes?

Whose laughter rings through all the house?
    Who always has a new cut bleeding?
Who can be quiet as a mouse,
    Who by my side, when I am reading,
A fair head leans? Who, with a kiss,
    Impulsive, sweet as April rain,
Will some half-risen doubt dismiss
    And lead me captive in his train?
Let all my years count up their treasure,
    This boy I love outweighs their measure.

Firelight

Now it is evening: draw the curtain close,
    The mist creeps round us from the grey hillside;
Here in the firelight let us think of those
    Far friends most with us in this eventide.

Do they at evening, in the camp-fire's glow,
    Pine for green fields seen from the cottage door,
Or sigh for all the country sights they know—
    How Autumn's beech leaves strew the valley's floor,

How the last apple on the topmost bough
    Glistens and reddens in the westering sun,
And hungry birds follow the heavy plough,
    And every chimney smokes with fires begun?

The hill that rises to the cloud-dark sky
    Is dearer still beneath the tropic blaze,
The lane that winds, the copse where rabbits lie
    Prick-eared in quick alarm, the frosty days

When the gay Hunt is up, on the lone veldt
    Grow lovelier in the exile's constant dream;
Oh England! where the wintry woods now melt
    In misty fields touched by the evening gleam!

Pile on the logs, among the rafters dark
    Send dancing shadows; here, at England's core,
We'll keep a welcome warm till they embark
    And knock with eager hands upon the door.

After Midnight

After midnight is passed and I hear the old clock below
Rumble and leisurely strike the hour of two,
When I am awake and see, like a drift of snow,
The moonlight cover our bed, I turn to you,

Loved face ethereal, faint in the dusk of your hair,
And gently, half-fearing to wake you, explore with my lips
The curve where the shadow lies deep and your throat lies bare,
And the earth and the moon and my soul are in total eclipse.

Then I am adrift in deep fear that it cannot last,
Since Love with his unclipped wings is so ready to fly.
O belovéd, if kisses were pinions to hold us fast,
No prisoners were ever so bound as you and I!

Now in the silence while earth turns eastward to dawn,
And stars grow fainter, and breathless night grows older,
And the elm tree's branches shadow the moonlit lawn,
I turn, and am soothed to sleep on your snow-white shoulder.

Middle Age

How quick the years are slipping by,
Spring blossom on the cherry bough,
A lark mounts up the April sky
And I am nearing fifty now.

How swift was love to set afire
The heart in other days of Spring,
The rapture and the fierce desire
To once experience everything!

How wide the world, what distant seas
Shone under Youth's enchanted heaven,
No realm so fabulous to appease
The wanderlust of twenty-seven!

Youth fearless, restless, brightly armed,
Ride forth and find what I have found,
The whole world narrowed to a charmed
Bird-haunted plot of English ground.

Of all this lovely earth one scene
I cherish most—this heritage
Where Spring comes now to make serene
These happier years of middle age.

The Veterans

Four old men by the haycart stand,
Each with a hayfork lending a hand,
Tossing the hay in the sunset glow
As they tossed it sixty years ago.

Said Charlie Sharp, nigh eighty-nine,
'Haycrops these days aren't as fine!',
Said old Mark Harman, eighty-five,
'Nor mown as well as with a scythe.'

Said old James Rixon, eighty-two,
'Nothing's the same, nor me, nor you!'
'Speak for yourself!' cried Reuben Pace,
And tossed a forkful in its place.

Seated by chairs at the cottage door
Where the pear tree grows on the wall, their four
Old wives talk in the evening sun—
One ninety, one eighty, two eighty-one.

*In Memoriam

(*Marchesa Nadja Malacrida*)

No sound not even leaf-fall breaks the spell
Where moonlight moves its shadows down the lawn;
    Oh watch you well,
Tall poplars, burnished windows, dark clipped fir—
    Is there no sign of her?

Indoors the log fire whispers in the grate,
The clock ticks softly on the open desk;
    Relentless Fate,
Save Time and dying flame, does nothing stir?
    Is there no sign of her?

I call her name within the silent house,
And touch the book wherein she marked the page;
    She cut these boughs
Of russet beach, this purple lavender—
    Oh lovely signs of her!

Surely within my garden she will come,
Drawn to its scene by so much happiness?
    False voice be dumb!
While blossom breaks or bird sings, everywhere
    There is a sign of her!

*Louis Tissier
(*1913-1939*)

Shall I then mourn my loss
And bow myself in grief
Since the fresh, opening flower
Ne'er knew the withered leaf?
Yet little I can hold
In lieu of autumn's gold.

The Old Cottage

I came to the cottage
    Lifting the knocker high,
But when the last echo died
    Not a soul made reply.

Out of the porch overhead
    Flew a startled bird,
I knocked, as to waken the dead,
    Not a footfall stirred.

In the silence I heard the call
    Of a hidden thrush,
The old house slept; over all
    A deep noonday hush.

Was I a ghost at the door,
    A century late
Since quick feet crossed the floor,
    Life passed at the gate?

'Leave me to crumble,' it seemed
    The old cottage said,
'I am all that a lover dreamed,
    And my lover's dead.'

*A Garden Revisited

O ghosts in the garden, crowd me not, leave
Quiet in my heart, though I came here to grieve,
Though the flesh, long dissolved, and the spirit of days,
Are beyond resurrection, are beyond blame or praise.
I loved you, I loved you!—the homing heart cries,
Where the winter of Time mocks the lost summer skies;
Nessun maggior dolore . . . —irrevocably true
That sorrow of sorrows the Florentine knew.
The heart is a lonely land, how lonely, they know
Who foolishly linger, reluctantly go.

Inscriptions

*A Man Arose

(*For Winston Churchill*)

They would not listen, they would not heed,
Content, they offered word for deed,
In peace the British Lion slumbered,
Maybe its active days were numbered;
They dreamed, a much-bewildered nation,
Content to play a peaceful role
Of blind and happy isolation,
Though intrigue ran from Pole to Pole.
They smiled with tolerant humour while
A hate-crazed creature, master of lies,
With arm aloft, and throaty *Heil*,
Screamed at the soft democracies.
They listened while the blacksmith's son
Strutted and ranted, black-shirted, obese,
Threatened the world with dagger and gun,
Boasted of bayonets in ancient Rome,
And spat in the silly face of Peace.
Secure within their sea-girt home,
Protected by their ancient moat,
They put their trust in ballot box
And gave their Kingdom to the vote.
They saw the Irish watchtowers fall
That kept the sea-lanes to the West;
Impervious to repeated shocks
What matter, if, in spite of all,
England in peace could dream and rest?
But in that halcyon hour a voice
Shattered the scene of soft repose,
They heard compelled, and not from choice,
When in their midst a Man arose.

A man arose, in England sired,
And suckled by the young free West,

69

Of lineage proud, of blood inspired
That long gave England of its best—
Statesmen and captains, truculent, bold,
Hot in valour, in caution cold,
Masters of swift manœuvres, gay,
With lightning thrust of speech and sword;
At Blenheim and at Malplaquet
Appeared the valiant overlord
From whom, through the descending years,
Came, in a time of perilous need,
One who but promised 'blood, sweat, tears'
To serve them as a conquering creed.

From ancient days we can recall
How lovely is this land of ours,
Mellowed by centuries rich with lore,
The cottage home, the timbered hall,
The evening scent of garden flowers,
The yew tree by the Vicarage door,
The vane upon the slim church steeple
Caught in the setting sun's last fire,
The pews with prayer-books neatly spaced,
The special cushion for the Squire—
A land of easy-going people,
Slow, trusting, worthy, free, kind-faced,
Her ills were plenty, yet of these
None came from planned malignity,
She forward stepped by slow degrees,
Remodelling life with dignity,
And from her turmoil somehow wrought,
By free consent and timed concession,
What others oft so dearly bought
With bloody strife and forced possession.

Beside the churchyard wall, beneath
The tall elms in their summer leaf,

The War Memorial proclaims
Upon its base the local names
Of Jack and Henry, Fred and Bill,
Who left the meadow and the hill,
Closed with sad heart each cottage door
And, dying for England, in strange lands,
Home to each threshold came no more.
New flowers are left by loving hands,
Though mockery in that legend runs—
'They died that England still might live.'
And yet no mockery. Hark! the guns
Hammer the air, a fugitive
Bird of death falls down the sky,
Prey of some daring English youth
Who questions not his destiny,
And fights to give the legend truth.

They are redeemed these lads—the jest is dead,
'. . . nor fight for King and Country . . .' once they said;
At twenty thousand feet, in furious speed,
They now affirm their faith, with matchless deed,
Roar through the clouds, in lonely battle give
The splendour of their youth—so we may live.

Sometimes in loneliness, in lands afar,
Where the hot desert wind of Libya blows,
Upon the mountain heights where Grecian snows
Untrammelled lie beneath a watchful star,
Within their wooden hut or flimsy tent,
When at the Zero hour hope seems forlorn,
In their lone watch by day or night or dawn,
A voice uplifts them—the embodiment
Of all that England means, in that one name
Her loveliness, her freedom and her fame;
This voice calls to them as no other can,
The voice of one undaunted, peerless man,

Speaking those words, immortal, tempered, true—
'. . . so much owed by so many to so few . . .'—
That they uprise, renewed, with all their fears,
Bred of the long and weak, disgraceful years,
Dismissed, march forth and, if perchance they fall,
New ranks press on at their great leader's call;
Inspired, they see and hear a flag unfurled,
A clarion note that rings around the world.

Strange, that he had, perforce, so long to wait
Ere in his hands they placed the ship of State,
Calling him to command in that late hour
When almost she had foundered. Robbed of power,
Long scoffed at, other men of meaner sense
Might have rebuffed their tardy penitence.
'Sirs,' he might well have said, 'did I not say
The time will come when you will rue the day,
When all your soft surrenders will assume
The shape and substance of impending doom?'
But great in heart, scorning to make retort,
While they beseeched this very man they fought,
He took his sorry, sad inheritance,
And calling to a people long dismayed,
Fashioned the might, the swift omnipotence
Of England's youth in war's dread cavalcade;
In the dark, desperate hour, ringed with her foes,
God-given to match the need, a Man arose.

Master of the written word,
And greatly simple in his speech,
He spoke, and when the nation heard,
A flame leapt in the heart of each
Who knew that Valour was not dead,
That Honour, sleeping long, had risen,
That Faith its shroud of doubt had shed,
And, fearless, walked as from a prison,

Free in a land alert at last,
Where men stood up with strength renewed
To justify their honoured past,
And prove them of the Lion's brood.

From hamlets set by singing streams,
From Scottish moors and Yorkshire dales,
From those twin towns of youthful dreams
Where laughter rings in ancient halls,
From mountains on whose headland falls
The sunset-splendour crowning Wales,
From sleepy Devon homes, deep-set
In wooded combes, by rocky shores,
From lush, green-meadowed Somerset,
From Sussex downs and wind-swept moors,
And from those teeming hives of men,
Great cities rich with ancient trade,
They answering came, and marched again,
A grim and thunderous cavalcade;
And round the world, in lands far-flung,
Desert and veldt and wilderness,
Wherever they spoke the English tongue,
And knew the creed that free men cherish,
Neither with hate nor bitterness
They rose to fight lest Freedom perish.

O Lord enthroned, O pitying Christ!
Thou see'st a fair land sacrificed,
A valiant people holding breath
Beneath a screaming rain of death;
Unbowed, unbeaten in the hell
Of mine, torpedo, bomb and shell,
Around them ruin swiftly falls
On churches, towns, memorials
Whose loveliness a thousand years
Have touched with grace of mellowed age;

And yet above the blood, sweat, tears,
They write for Time a deathless page,
Affirm the holy spirit of Man
Transcends his mortal heritage.

Oh when that happier dawn shall break,
And from the land winged Death has flown,
When from the conflict they arise,
A nation through its suffering grown
To dauntless heights of sacrifice,
O Man of Sorrows, thrice-denied,
Give comfort to these, crucified,
Who long in faith and valour stood
To crush a monstrous creed of blood.

Inscription for a Garden Wall

(Commemorating Midshipman Edward Hodgson, R.N.,
killed, aged 17, at the Battle of Jutland, 1916, and his brother
Lieutenant John, aged 20, killed at Kut, 1917)

Stranger, pause here and think of us a while
Who loved this garden in our boyhood's days,
Brothers in death as life, whom many a mile
Has sundered; for amid the pathless ways
Where northern waters roll, one rests, and one
Sleeps in the desert 'neath a tropic sun.

Laugh softly, children, in your mirth for we
Were once as you; remember us who knew
The golden summer noon, who loved to see
The moon upon the roses, and the dew;
Remember us, and leave a votive sigh;
It was for England we went forth to die.

*Entering Mons

(*Armistice Day, November 11th, 1918*)

The drums roll loudly down the streets,
A thousand flags stream in the sun,
The liberated city greets
With one long roar the men who won
In that last hour of agony
The victor's palm, who in long days
And nights of quenchless gallantry,
Nameless, gave all for Britain's praise.

And while the morning air resounds
With cries of triumph, while the Square
Surges with faces to the bounds
Four-walled, where yet again appear
From window, balcony and roof
Faces and flags and waving hands,
A coloured warp that threads the woof
Of men that march to rhythmic bands—

Tearful, with vision blurred, I feel
The presence of a greater host,
And see the shadowy ranks that reel
But break not where the iron boast
Of the enraged invader falls
Upon the dauntless English few;
Where the triumphant trumpet calls
The old brigades march with the new.

You have not slept, you could not sleep,
But now in wonderful array,
Unseen, your proud battalions sweep
Across the plain of Mons today,
In one last march to hear awhile
The cheers of those for whom you died,

Worn warriors, greeted mile on mile
With hearts that break to see your pride.

Marching you came, a soundless throng,
Was it the wind passed down the street?
Bannered you passed, and all along
The cheering crowd grew hushed, the beat
Of marching men was felt, not heard;
We knew your presence, holding breath,
Senses acute, divinely stirred,
We saw the legion led by Death.

*Captain Albert Ball, V.C., D.S.O., M.C.
(1896–1917)

Twenty his years, gay, fearless, kind, he fought,
Knew Death as a familiar, bound his brows
With laurel, an Olympian soul, nor sought
The honourable rest which Fame allows,
But, godlike, 'mid his foes, in his last fight
Above the sunset glow, passed from our sight.

*So Immortal a Flower

*(Epitaph for a memorial to the British
soldiers fallen in Crete, 1941)*

To have fought, to have lost, to have fallen,
To have won from the losing such glory,
Under a rain of Death so immortal a flower to have planted,
In the hush of the even that falls
When the strife of the day is a story,
In the breaking of waves will their voices sound o'er a sea enchanted;
Here shall we boast how their valour gained them a raiment immortal,
Listen, and grieve, and be proud
Where, deathless, they passed the Portal.

Burial of the Unknown Soldier

(Westminster Abbey, November 11th, 1920)

They carry him, unknown, all-honoured, slowly
　　Through multitudes made free by his lost name;
In the dim sanctuary he lies now, lowly,
　　Companioned by the dead of mighty fame;
The muffled drums beat for him, he hears not,
　　The martial tread of feet can wake him never;
Nor, could he speak or hear, for this rare spot
　　Would he give thanks, but only—'Vain endeavour!
Nothing I want now, being past your giving—
　　What of my comrades, fare they well in living?'

The Lamps are Lit

The lamps are lit in Henley Town
    And mistily flows the stream,
But there's one lad no more returning
    To his home and the firelit dream.

The houses lean together still
    And the gables shadow the street,
But there's one voice will sound no more there
    By the bridge where the lovers meet.

The owl cries in the Fawley woods,
    And the moon's over Remenham Hill,
But one lad goes not a-courting
    By the race of Hambledon Mill.

The lamps are out in Henley Town,
    And it's dawn in Bu Saadeth
Where a comely lad lies a-sleeping
    In a slumber that draws no breath.

*Futility

They send me, Charles, long letters on your death,
Full of fair phrases culled from poetry
That do not blind me—let them save their breath;
The nectared lies of immortality,
The sounding rhetoric, the pompous phrase,
The talk of 'supreme sacrifice', the 'great
Reward'—what are these 'gainst your withered days,
Your dear lost face, the squalor of your fate?
That you were brave, I know, but still you clung
To life that meant so much; they say you cried
In that last hour, feeling you were so young,
And desperately fought for life, and died.
These letters, Charles, they mock me with their lies,
Their borrowed phrases that belittle life
And love and laughter—I can see your eyes
As once they glowed, your body like a knife
Tempered and flashing in a summer sea,
Or hear your voice enraptured over books,
Or in the bathroom singing merrily
At early morn, and days in river nooks
And tennis sets—these memories all seem
Like ghosts that haunt your room now you are gone,
And make me think your end is but a dream,
How can it be the end—at twenty-one?
But when I read these letters then I know
You will not come again, nor does their praise
Lighten the heaviness of this great blow;
I cannot kiss your brow, nor see the place
Where they have left you; as they write of 'fame',
Your 'splendid gift', my only thought is this—
What will they care ten years hence for your name,
Who cares a damn who died at Salamis?

Epitaph

(*For L. B. R., Lieutenant, R.A.*
Killed, North Africa, May 2nd, 1943, aged 22)

Ον οι θεοι φιλοῦσιν ἀπθνῄσκι νέος

It may be again that Life will mould a young face
To break a heart with in some new day unseen,
But never again, for one, can return the grace
That was yours, dear Lucien, beyond Fate's malice serene.

Lucien: In Memoriam

I

'Within the sonnet's narrow plot of ground
Shakespeare unlocked his heart,' and daring, I,
With lesser skill have walked in it and found,
Recalling memories, lost felicity—
Some moment of you, transient, yet bound
In Time's immortal book—how you would lie
Bare-limbed upon the lawn; the happy sound
Of laughter when youth laughs and knows not why.
Let me then write, ere memory fades; perchance
Others shall glean a glimpse of boyhood's grace,
And know in what sweet bondage I was kept;
Let me recall how in your sunny glance
My heart was light, and when your eager face
Turned to me laughing, how my fond heart leapt.

2

I saw you first in an enchanted place,
Venice imperial, on her wide lagoon,
Whose light and beauty glowed in your young face;
Along the Grand Canal you came one noon,
No gondolier more skilled than you whose boat
Skimmed the green flood, a golden child, eleven,
Sandalled, in brief blue shorts, chrome-yellow coat,
Your tumbling hair blond 'neath the azure heaven;
A child of the lagoon yet Scotland's own,
Exiled by Fate, in the strange way of things
Inheriting the loving care I gave;
I, too, great harvest reaped from little sown;
What music in a house a child's voice brings
Whereby the master soon becomes the slave!

84

3

Lovely the cottage in the summer noon,
Lovely the Thames with swans upon her breast,
Lovely the beachwoods and the lazy croon
Of doves around the dovecote. High the crest
Of larchwoods where, on summer nights, the moon
Rises, all golden, climbing heavenwards; best,
The stars above the poplar trees that soon
Will cease to rustle in a world at rest.
Then through the dormer window moonlight falls
Upon a sleeping boy, to touch his head
With silver, and his smooth young cheek to kiss,
And, while up in the woods a lone owl calls,
Creeps softly where he slumbers in his bed
Drawing quiet breath, deep-pillowed in his bliss.

4

I have no son but all a father knows
Of love and love's reward is surely mine
When your impulsive boyish spirit shows,
In the quick joy that makes your eyes to shine,
In some shy gesture, or slow smile that flows
Over me till my fond heart laughs with thine;
My own most surely since our union grows,
Wanting no fleshly tie to make divine.
And so in you I find myself again,
Retrieve the wasted years, my youth renew,
And know once more the peace of thoughtless days,
And wipe from memory's palimpsest each stain:
So, in your innocent eyes, your lips' bright hue,
Fair hair, smooth brow, I find my boyhood's face.

5

Now ruthless Time has counted seventeen years
And, grown a youth, to manhood hurrying on,
I see you, tall and slender, and my fears
Grow fast for soon your boyhood will be gone:
No more the rippling laughter, welling tears,
The mouth that quivered and the eyes that shone,
The coronal of grace a boy's head wears—
Too swiftly comes your world of twenty-one.
O foolish heart to hoard each trivial thing—
Unbuttoned shirt, loose tie, scarred chubby knee,
The shoes sent flying, clothes flung anywhere,
The flooded floor as from the bath you spring,
And, daring me to catch you, wildly flee;
And, oh, your pillowed head and tumbling hair!

6

June's heaven of blue, the silver Thames, tall trees
Motionless in the slumbering summer's day,
And golden in the noon a Grecian frieze
Of youths who by the river's green bank play;
There you stand, naked, while an errant breeze
Ripples the river's face and dies away—
So in the Stoa stood young Charmides;
You dive, and round you breaks the silver spray.
Supple, sun-tanned, with head of wet gold hair,
Amid your gay companions, laughter-loud,
You throw a challenge, and the race is on.
Now you regain the bank and, standing there,
I see a group against a sunlit cloud—
The deathless riders of the Parthenon.

They say there is a star at every birth
That sets the pattern of our mortal life;
If so it be, is then the effort worth
What gain may come from our predestined strife?
I ask the question. Is this troubled earth
With famine, pestilence, wars, and earthquakes rife,
A game the high gods play, a moment's mirth
Ere falls upon the victim's throat the knife?
Twice in our generation we have seen
The youth of England slaughtered; is the price
Final, or shall we see it asked anew?
Vainly I brood upon what might have been,
Since desert sands saw your dire sacrifice.
There ends the dream: Lucien, aged twenty-two.

Miscellaneous

*The Golden Journey from Samarkand

(*In memory of James Elroy Flecker, 1884–1915*)

Scarcely has set the moon, whose bland
White face shone over Samarkand,
Ere sounds the voice of the khan keeper,
A heavy drinker, a light sleeper.

Arise! awake! the dawn breaks clear at last,
The song of pilgrims on the highway grows.
Hearken! the goatherd with his flock goes past,
The misty sun stands on the mountain snows.

Arise! arise! O Masters, while the morn
Is cool for pilgrim feet that journey forth,
Oh pleasant is the way at early dawn;
Go, seek adventure, East and West and North.

Allah be with you, Masters, fare you well,
God's Prophet give you peace in wandering,
And guide your last steps with his fatal bell
To that Great Khan where moon-white houris sing.

The Pilgrims, poor, ill-shod and bare,
Shiver in the cold mountain air.

Always we seek the city just beyond
The far horizon on the valley's rim,
Pilgrims are we to distant Trebizond;
Allah will lead us though our sight is dim.

Strangers have told us how, in great Stamboul,
A hundred minarets climb to the sky,
Like stars that glimmer bright in Heaven's pool—
Allah will show this wonder ere we die.

A Merchant, going forth to sell and buy,
Crowds, with his camels, the caravanserai.

A hundred minarets, a hundred domes,
Rise in the City by the Golden Horn;
Rich is the earth to him who ever roams,
Who journeys not, the same is never born.

These eyes of mine saw Mecca many years,
These feet know well the ways of old Baghdad,
The world's a home to him who never fears,
Who knows the will of Allah and is glad.

A Boy with piping voice, red-lipped and slim,
Turns where the mountains in the haze are dim.

They say beyond the mountains is a sea
That breaks in diamonds at their purple feet,
And curls in foam, a silver filigree,
All shadowed as the wind across the wheat.

Men sail its waters in their lateen boats,
Along strange shores they creep, and in the night
Watch the high mountain's crest that dimly floats
Behind them, and at dawn is out of sight.

An Old Man, bleary-eyed, loose-mouthed, and yellow,
Jeers at the boy; an evil-faced old fellow.

Youth has a fever in its blood! No more
For me the dusty road, I am grown old,
This journey ends in home; I have great store
Of merchandise to sell for goodly gold;

Twelve caravans are mine all filled with things
Guarded by eunuchs armed with gleaming swords,
Each holds a fair Circassian maid who sings
And wakes desire in hearts of wealthy lords.

A Young Prince in rich raiment, languid, waves
His jewelled hand, and forward march his slaves.

Far have I travelled, filled with great unrest,
When o'er the valley rises the new moon
I shall have reached the garden I love best
That flowers above the city of Samsoon.

There wait my concubines, and singing boys
With cheeks of rose and brows of alabaster;
There will be pleasure in the cry and noise—
'See! on the door the shadow of our Master!'

Two Beggars see the travellers coming nigh
And energetically twitch and cry.

Alms, we beseech you, Masters, many prayers
We make for pilgrims, which the Prophet heeds.
Alms, we beseech you, Masters, may long years
Reward you for your charitable deeds!

But all their filth and twitching brings them naught,
Yet many prayers they made—though of a sort.

Curses upon you! Every plague and pest
Be yours! May blindness take your eyes, and thieves
Your purses! Miserable dogs! No rest
Be yours! May Hell's winds chase you like old leaves!

A Youth sings, working in the harvest fields;
Supple and bronzed, a shining scythe he wields.

93

In Trebizond there lived a king,
A thousand years ago,
Who loved a maiden sweet as Spring
When almond blossoms blow.

She passed his palace day by day
When dawn came o'er the hills:
For love of her he pined away—
Vain love the bravest kills.

Though kings have gifts from many hands
And lords of life are they,
Yet love obeys no man's commands
And goes its wilful way.

In Trebizond there lived a king
A thousand years ago;
O Maiden unto whom I sing,
His royal grief I know!

A Scholar speaks, his eyesight dim with toil,
Long years 'mid scrolls of parchment, seeking spoil.

What man desires too much, oft Allah gives,
That which he seeks, he finds in bitterness,
Fulfilment is the death of all that lives,
The happier he is who seeks the less.

Knowledge has mocked me, brothers, many years,
The beggars in their wretchedness are wise,
The thought of Whence and Whither breeds but fears,
Wisdom most sure becomes the dupe of lies.

A rich Jew, with long fingers manicured,
Grown bitter with the scorn he has endured.

What is the gain of wise men when they learn
That logic leads them to a barren end?
I serve the proven law—the thrifty earn
Power to take in bondage fools who spend.

'Allah provides!' the beggars cry, yet know
They are unheeded as the desert sand;
Tell them to place their trust in Allah, show
The beggars you believe—with empty hand!

> *A Poet, who, while travelling long roads,*
> *Beguiles the time by chanting Hafiz' Odes.*

Yet falls the rose that hoarded its perfume,
Life gives one spring to spend and, spent or saved,
No prayers, no wealth avail man to illume
With youthful faith the old heart, grief-engraved.

'Tis better far be spendthrift with the joy
That ends too soon, to kiss the lips of youth,
Laugh lover-like, and every hour employ
Spilling the rich red wine with little ruth.

> *A Lover, who can laugh at all the wise*
> *Old men who seek the Prophet's Paradise.*

One Paradise I know, to stand at dusk
Beneath the cherry blossom with a maid
Whose hair is odorous with myrrh and musk,
Whose brow gleams like a moon above the glade,

To feel her soft young bosom rise and fall,
Twin lilies floating in a secret pool,
My lips adventuring to savour all,
And in my hair her fingers white and cool.

A Soldier, strong, who with his sturdy arm
Held off much peril, to him much charm.

Better the camp beneath the frosty stars,
The choice of women in the captured town
At the day's end—how oft the door unbars
To him who has the soldier's deft renown!

Ah, let us live, too soon we may be dead,
A gnat can dance above a slain man's nose,
And vultures pick the eyes out of his head;
Tomorrow I am here, or gone—who knows?

A calm Philosopher, who disapproves
Logic that does not run in the old grooves.

Philosophy, my son, philosophy
Alone endures. Study the life of man
And learn how Allah—

A Cynic, one who never puts away
Temptation when a wineshop bids him stay.

Bah! friend, believe me,
Grown old in folly, 'tis a better plan

Never to think, but follow Fancy's lead,
Be poet in the art of life not words,
Love where you will, and eat when comes the need,
That's wisdom scorned by fools but known to birds!

And now 'tis sunset and the pilgrims halt
Before the gates of Trebizond, the salt
Sea wind blows chilly on the darkening track;
'Tis good to hear the porter's cry and see the gates roll back.

The Pilgrims

Allah in our journeyings
Guides us through the ways of Death,
Yet to gates of Life he brings
All who know the truths He saith;
Long the pilgrim-trek has been,
Yet in faith the end was seen.

A Woman, old and thin,
Peers as they pass in.

Fifty! all strangers, and not one
Has the face of my lost son.

The last gleam of sunset goes,
The great gates close.

*To Shelley, after seeing Ozymandias

I, too, a traveller in an antique land,
Have looked on Ozymandias, king of kings,
And read his boastful lines above the sand;
Under the timeless stars his challenge rings,
And naught remains save two stone trunkless limbs;
Not vain his boast; the Mighty should despair
Since your immortal voice his folly hymns
With words that flower in the desert air.

To W.A.C., on his twenty-first birthday

Now like a ship launched on the golden tide,
Festooned with flags amid the ringing cheers,
You sail, well-speeded, to adventurous seas
Gleaming before you in the uncharted years.
Whether to ports in golden climes you go,
Where new enchantments crowd the thronging hours,
Or, fate-bound, touch dark shores where men are tried
Unto the utmost limit of their powers,
One wish I have, one prayer on your behalf,
Be short or long the voyage you shall make—
Courage be yours, and that supreme content
Founded in honour no man can wreck or break.

Madonna and Child

(For the Marqués Santo Domingo's fifteenth-century painting)

God was Thy father, but the hand of Man
Infant, hath surely made Thee twice divine—
The enamelled flowers and the green-plumed bird
Attend Thee, on the breast of Her whose shrine
Glows now before us. Death twice finds defeat,
Since the transcendent love enfolds Thee, child,
And the immortal brush of one long dead
Keeps Thee from Time's contagion, undefiled.

Bells and Silks and Ivory

Little Lilian laughs at me
But I cannot guess the joke—
Why do things seem funnier
When unknown to other folk?
What the secret is she hides,
And why she laughs so merrily,
No one knows. To me it seems
A fairy schooner slowly rides
On a moonlit pearl-bright sea
With a cargo full of dreams,
Bells and silks and ivory,
When little Lilian laughs at me.

Homecoming

Cliffs breaking through the haze,
  And a narrowing sea,
Soon will my eager gaze
  Have sight of thee,

England, the lovelier now
  For absence long,
Soon shall I see your brow,
  Hear a lark's song.

Heart, curb your beating—there
  Channel cliffs glow,
Eddystone, Plymouth, where
  Drake mounts the Hoe!

Red of the Devon loam,
  Green of the hills,
April! and I am home,
  God, my heart thrills!

Far have I travelled and
  Great beauty seen,
But oh, out of England
  Is anywhere green?

Thankful and thankful again
  As never before,
One of the Englishmen
  Comes to his shore!

*Nicoletta

(*For Nicoletta Panni*)

When Nicoletta sings
I hear a hundred things—
Birds in the woodland,
Canaries in cages,
And wild March winds along the shore
Where the sea rages.

When Nicoletta sings
I recall a thousand things—
The dream that a young boy
Knew in enchanted Springs,
And, not forgotten, the sorrow, the joy
That filled the years,
Returning now
With love bedimmed with tears—
When Nicoletta sings.

Le Comte de St Clair

(*Étude de Chopin*)

Etienne Hyacinthe, *petit* Comte de St Clair,
On a piano stool sat, little feet in the air,
With glossy neat shoes, and white *pantalon*,
At a black Erard Grand in a long, grey *salon.*
The great shining lid was upraised in the air
Reflecting a boy with wavy blond hair,
Reflecting myself, and his *chère Maman,*
In a French-windowed villa in old Avignon;
Half-closed *persiennes* kept the room in cool shade
But the white keys gleamed as the little boy played.
He had asked, so gravely,—'*Maman, que veux-tu?*'
—'*L'Étude de Chopin—Je l'aimerais beaucoup!*'
Then over the keys the young fingers ran,
Playing the *Première Étude* with the greatest *élan,*
And I still can remember, through fifty years gone,
That small boy with black shoes and white *pantalon;*
And wherever a Grand lifts its lid in the air,
And whoever plays Chopin, I hear everywhere
That child with his bright face and wavy blond hair,
Etienne Hyacinthe, *petit* Comte de St Clair.

Mr Smith in Venice

The pigeons strut, the tourists talk
At cafés in the shining Square,
Heavenwards the Campanile soars,
An arrow in the azure air.
The four bronze horses lift in vain
Their fetlocks where St Mark's, agleam
In oriental splendour, sits,
While over the Rialto stream
Such crowds as never Shylock knew;
But Mr Smith, perspiring, sighs,
Indifferent to Palladio,
For Myrtle Villas, Kensal Rise.

Mr Smith in the Turkish Bath

How beautiful the body of that youth,
Firm-thighed, flat-bellied, a poem of the flesh;
My belly, like a hairy gooseberry ripe;
My veins on sunken flanks a purple mesh;
And yet, perhaps, my Saviour sees me young,
My soul, prayer-disciplined, a thing of grace,
While that young stallion, flesh-tormented, strives
Against the bridle checking Youth's hot pace.

Mr Smith on Marriage

There was a time when I was quite a dandy
And went the pace on women, horses, brandy,
And many a jolly girl thought me a lad,
(What fun in Paris with Colette I had!)
But Mabel Dodge, our local lawyer's daughter,
Had a nice dowry, and with luck I caught her.
Luck—after forty years I still say luck—
The golden goose I caught has proved a duck.

Mr Smith in Heaven

How strange, he thought, surveying Heaven's plain,
Thereon to dwell through all Eternity,
That once he raged because he missed a train—
The homeward four-fifteen in Fifty-three.

*Lines for the unveiling of Haydn's portrait by Fuseli

(at Mrs Murray Crane's, Fifth Avenue, New York)

Here now I greet you, in a far domain,
By Fuseli's brush made visible to your sight,
Dear gentle friends, gathered by Mrs Crane
To celebrate my transatlantic flight.

Here in a room beneath whose windows roars
The traffic of Manhattan's avenue,
A ghost from other *salons*, whose applause
Still sounds within my ears, I'll play to you.

Let me, then, from my eighteenth century bring
To yours, distracted by the world's unrest,
A little music, light and lingering,
To give a soothing respite to your breast.

Mine was an age of candles on the spinet,
The violin's plaint, the 'cello's low lament,
And sighs to close each music-laden minute—
Have you, for all your progress, such content?

*Lines Completed

1

How odd
Of God
To choose
The Jews.
Then,
With more hope,
He chose
The Pope.

2

Twinkle, twinkle, little star,
How I wonder what you are!
Lady, since you wrote this verse
Man's unscrewed the Universe,
Leaving little else to know;
Your twinkling star's just H_2O.

3

O what a tangled web we weave,
When first we practise to deceive!
The flame of Truth is never cold,
The liar forgets the lie he told.

4

A line has length without breadth, said Euclid.
A sermon of length without depth is putrid,
But the teller of tales that have length without end,
To Euclid's axiom adds terror, my friend.

The plural of house is houses.[1]
But the plural of mouse isn't mouses,
For its plural's the same as a louse's;
And you cannot have singular trousers—
How elusive grammatical nous is!

[1]Nesfield's *English Grammar*

The Torch

Twin castles stand in Sion,
Above the icy Rhône,
And morning makes the mountains
Her shining throne;
Who walks these streets of Sion,
The peasants of Valais,
Or the men who marched with Caesar
The imperial way?

Two thousand years in Sion
Are shrunk to one tense hour
When Pierre of the vineyard,
Jehanne, like a flower,
Mingle their strength and beauty,
Two peasants of Valais,
Passing the torch of passion
That fuses clay.

How can we, foolish cyphers,
Believe our faltering hands
Shall guide the line Fate traces,
Delay Time's sands?
Two thousand years of Sion
In Pierre's lovelit eyes
Light the undying passion,
And gird his thighs.

*The Priest of Sant' Ambrogio

(*Seeking Max Beerbohm*)

The priest of Sant' Ambrogio
Was a little man and young,
Out of the shadow of an olive tree,
Like a small, quick gnome, he had sprung,
Black in the pool of moonlight
Flooding the cobbled little Square,
While I wondered if he lived in this century,
And he wondered what I was doing there.

Far below lay the bay of Rapallo
In a crescent of lights along the sea,
And the fireflies flitted in the night air,
While each sentinel cypress tree
Stood guard, very upright and important,
Determined not a moonbeam should pass,
And the little frogs in leafy dells of water
Croaked a tuneless chorus hidden in the grass.

The priest of Sant' Ambrogio
Doffed his broad-brimmed hat of felt,
Very small beneath the glimmering *campanile*,
He might have been a shadow that would melt
In the first bright beam of sunrise,
But his voice was a human one, and clear,
Gentle, with a boy's treble in it—
A little glad, he seemed, of someone near.

If he understood ten words of my Italian
When I said, '*Buona sera, Signore*,'
'Twas no more than I could gather of his English,
But his hands helped out the sense he would convey.
He bowed, responded, clearly comprehending
I had lost the route along the cobbled tracks—

Down the mountainside, there, on the highway,
Dwelt *L'illustrissimo signore*, Beerbohm Max.

The priest of Sant' Ambrogio will grow old, and one day I
Shall no more climb mountain mule-tracks
Where the cypress stands on guard, against the sky;
He will tend his flock and hear their last confessions,
Doze and totter, but will always be for me
A shadow, by the olives in the moonlight,
On a small piazza high above the sea.

On the beach, Alassio

Children, the happy sounds you make
Are as the cries of flitting birds
That 'mid these palms and olives shake
Their coloured wings, and though your words,
Birdlike, no sense to me convey,
Such music is your happiness
I need not know the things you say—
Words have their magic none the less.

The turquoise sea in idleness
Suffers no tide to urge its flow,
But throws a green, translucent veil
Around your dancing feet. Aglow
In this Italian noon, your frail
Innocent beauty crowns the hours,
And when the evening shadows creep
Across the terraced vines, like flowers
You will be folded up in sleep.

Vladimir de Pachmann: a memory

(*Schloss Esterház*)

His old piano is dumb forever,
The dust lies thick on the ivory keys,
For the Master is dead, his fingers will never
Touch them again, and the melodies,
The tender old pieces he loved to play,
The Chopin *Berceuse*, the *Barcarolle*,
Went with him when he passed away—
What music in heaven will cheer his soul?

None, I warrant, as good as he made
When we sat so still in this long white room,
Watching his hands 'neath the candle shade,
And the fine old head in the evening gloom.
A *Ballade* of Chopin's flowed out from those fingers,
We saw in the dusk young lovers in rapture,
We heard their vows, where the melody lingers,
And then their sighs, which the last notes capture.

Or maybe a Schumann trifle came after—
What a whirlwind of notes took flight as he played,
Silvery-toned as a maiden's laughter,
Whence had it come, and how was it made?
Then, suddenly, after the laughter, came thunder,
The octaves woke in the bass and roared,
And chaos grew as we watched in wonder
Those frail hands crash out chord on chord.

And then, as the sunshine follows the storm,
The right hand rippled high up in the treble,
And the birds sang out, and the air grew warm,
While a minor note, like a falling pebble,
Dived down through the flowing music and sank
With a sound familiar to all who ever
Threw a stone from a river's bank.
Can it be that enchantment has vanished forever?

So Browning . . .

Grow old along with me
The best is yet to be,
The last of life
    for which the first was made:

Did Browning believe it?
I cannot conceive it,
        for not such a fool was he—
The loss of wife,
That last decade
        dragged out with gossip and tea?
Still, the gesture was fine;
We can always admire
The well-sounding line
Brave old Browning sang to his lyre!

Camels in the snow

New York to Springfield, on we go
Through woodlands white with sunlit snow,
Through gaunt plantations where each tree
Marches in black solemnity,
And, suddenly, the speeding train
Slips through a town and out again,
Through factory labyrinths, new made,
Vast temples to Man's great god, Trade.
Then loneliness once more, where show
Brown woodlands sharp against the snow,
Grim skeletons of barren boughs;
And here and there a lonely house,
Wood-built, proclaims a nearing town;
Now, through my window, slowing down,
I see a thing that would provoke
Laughter, were grief a fitting joke—
There, tethered in a bleak backyard,
Six camels stand upon a hard
White frozen pond and, 'mid the ice,
Long for a desert paradise.

Poor slaves of men whom business guides
To offer you for children's rides,
Not yours the only tragedy
In Life's queer-stocked menagerie!
For as my train, fast gathering speed,
Runs by, upon a sign I read
DEVON, and in a moment I
Am dreaming of an English sky,
Dreaming of Bideford, where ride
The fishing boats adown the tide,
Of Lynton, Lynmouth, and a score
Of hamlets on a rock-bound shore.

New York to Springfield—on we go;
Laugh not at camels in the snow.

*Strip Poker. Harvard, 1920

The snow is thick in the moonlit Quad,
And here we sit and play,
Ten lads nigh naked in a room
Hot as a Roman day.
What would your father think, Larry,
What would your mother say,
To see their blue-eyed boy go down
The alcoholic's way?
Round goes the bottle, slam go the cards,
Naked as he was born,
Hank, having lost on one mad fling,
Becomes a Grecian faun;
And Spud, a giant six-foot two,
A wizard on the track,
Has wildly risked his all and lost
The shirt upon his back;
Homer, with only white 'briefs' left,
Plays with a grim intent—
Strange, if that lad should one day be
His country's President!
Fate plays a hand as strange as any—
A Judge of the Supreme Court
May one day sit on a backside spanked
Because his credit was short.

Oh, boys, remember mother's prayer,
This is no way to fame,
Let's cork the bottle and find our clothes
And end the boozy game.
The moon is full above the river,
The night is still and clear,
Put on your shorts and let us run,
Breathing the cold, pure air,
Along the shining River Charles,
Then, breathless, pause, and stand

Where Longfellow heard on the midnight bridge
The clocks on either hand,
And mused, with thoughts of Life and Death
To which the bells gave tongue:
Too soon we shall be frail and old,
Tonight, thank God, we're young!

The Mouse

The little mouse watched
Then ran over the floor,
The woman with the big feet
Went out of the door.

The little mouse sat
On his hind legs thin,
And his sharp black eyes
Took all things in—

The curtains drawn,
The old man on the bed,
Whose eyes did not move
In his ashen head,

The worn hands folded
Upon his chest,
The watch, still ticking,
He once possessed.

The little mouse listened,
The little mouse ran,
Alone in a room
With a death-still man.

*Arrival in Venice

The Grand Canal. So here's a dream come true!
A few yards more, the station's at our back,
We're out of Europe, on another planet.
A turn, some steps, green water at our feet,
Then 'Gondola, signore?' 'Per piacere.'
And we embark. What, did we dream it all,
Do we dream now? No! Pictures did not lie,
Nor love songs, nor the theatre-set, 'tis all
As if we knew it well. Surely we'll see,
Where the Canal bends sharply, the Rialto,
The high-arched bridge, the quay where Shylock walked,
Antonio blustered, and the reputed house
Of Desdemona—though she never knew it!
This gondola is almost coffin-like,
So black, so sombre in this riotous town,
Yet somehow right, now once we've seen it so.
The church there, with the water at its steps—
It's so familiar! Through that marble door
A Cardinal will come, red-tassel-hatted,
If we but wait a moment—Santa Madonna!
(Excitement makes me lapse into Italian
As once I spoke it when, in my old palace,
I gave a banquet to the Doge, when Titian
Had finished the new fresco in the salon)
Why, that's the Palazzo— But, it's all palazzi,
(The plural ends in 'i', my love. Just lend me
The Baedeker a moment) every side!
We'll come back here in moonlight, see it slowly.
What did he say? Palazzo Vendramin?
Isn't it glorious, early Renaissance,
And with what columns and expanse of glass!
That's how a palace should be. Do you wonder
Wagner returned to die there? I remember
D'Annunzio wrote of it in Il Fuoco;
A Bourbon owns it now—how like a Bourbon!

This gondola moves dog-wise, the steel prow
Rides like a swan's neck high above the water,
Exactly as we've seen it in a film,
A moon above, and lovers in delirium.
And so are we, my darling! Can't I kiss you?
What if the gondolier should see? How often
He's steered the love-lost through a shining dream!
Oh look, my own! The pointed-gothic windows,
Like flowers of stone, with open balconies
That seem to glow still from their load of beauty,
The red-haired women Titian loved, who waved,
Greeting gallants, young, gay, in scarlet hose,
Rowed by their *gondolieri* to San Marco.
Now, we are rowed there! Dearest, can we ever
Go back to Onslow Gardens, catch a bus,
And tell the char to take a pint of milk?

*A Ghost of Venice

There walks the Countess Guiccioli!
Is she flesh or legend now,
She whose face the long-dead poet
Looked upon, whose girlish brow
Such tresses, dark as midnight, crowned—
'Tis her very ghost, I vow!

Yes—there is a note still lingers
Of the voice that answered when
That proud head, on such a bosom,
Lay, the poet-lord whose pen
Held enslaved the whole of Europe;
Yes, it sounds, I think, as then.

Once, and only once, I saw them,
On a far-off April day,
In a *salon* set in Venice,
Off the Grand Canal. They say
'Twas that very night enslaved them,
Till he went the war-like way.

Ah, he was a man, *per Dio*!
Such a head to look upon,
Proud, and with a flash of spirit
That, though forty years have gone,
I recall the thrill that swept us
Seeing then the Destined One.

Oh, they gossiped, but 'twas Venice,
Truth or tale, it mattered not,
'La, Lord Byron!' cried the lady,
'Not another word!'—and what
The story was, we'll never know,
That left the lady's face so hot.

Yes, he was a charmer. Wicked?
Well, depends on where you are!
Maybe sin's romance in Venice,
Istanbul or Zanzibar.
Venice is the gate, remember,
Of the East, where rules Ishtar.

Not that I support the rumour,
Let us watch it, you and I,
That we are not less than human,
Else, being caught, we may not cry
On the world to pity frailty;
Others judged them, never I!

Sixteen years, such girlish beauty
Breaking into blossom then,
He so handsome, with a manner
Placing him apart from men—
How they talked and laughed and parted,
Sighed 'Arrivederci' when

Came the gondolier to take her,
Gliding down the starlit water,
Sitting at her side the husband,
Hateful, old and rich, who bought her,
Just a child, sweet, knowing only
What the convent nuns had taught her.

Do you marvel that, impatient,
Her young wings spread out to take
Such a flight in Love's dominion
As they only know who make
Full surrender to the moment,
Ruthless of the bonds they break?

Byron, wearied with philandering,
Had not been the world's applauded
And escaped the world's loud censure—
'Tis a way the much rewarded
Suffer for the light upon them;
Yet the end, it is accorded,

Fitted well the baffled eagle.
Do you think she said him Nay
When he found a cause to die for?
Lips that loved did not cry 'Stay!'
All his purpose hers, so found he
Night awhile and deathless day.

Yes, a ghost of the young countess,
Beauty, Youth, all gone with Time,
But there's something she's denied it—
Safe within a book of rime
Live and glow the hours immortal
Born of that sweet, southern clime.

*Cimarosa
(1749–1801)

'Neath your window, Cimarosa,
In Venice, on a warm June night,
Where the *campanile* throws a
Shadow on the Square, moon-bright,
I thought I heard a strain, a ghost
Of sound that on a breeze went by;
O *Maestro*, for a moment, almost
I sought you on your balcony!

Seemed then, from that *salon* dim
Whose windows look upon the Square,
From your clavichord a whim
Of music took the summer air—
A new trifle, duet, trio,
Setting for Goldoni's text?
Tell me, dear Domenico—
The Fenice craves your next!

Gone—and now the Square is quiet,
Two black cats are all that's seen;
On your balcony a riot
Of geraniums, red and green,
Glimmering in the moonlight. Can
Nigh two hundred years have fled
Since, oh tuneful-fingered man,
You struck those chords that are not dead?

*Giardino Eden, Venice

(*Written in the album of Princess Alexander of Greece,
at her villa, on the Giudecca, Venice*)

Eden, they say, was lost to weeping Eve,
And Adam sweated for that mortal sin,
But had they found your garden, I believe,
A paradise by the lagoon, walled in,
They would have known how cypress and how vine,
How sun and moon and stars, in a divine
Concomitance, bring to our wondering eyes
All they had loved in their lost Paradise.

To H.H. in Venice

When fall the autumn leaves and life turns grey,
Will you remember
One far Venetian day
In warm September,
When by the *fondamento, ponte, rio,*
We walked, a trio,
Where Titian and Bellini built their fame
'Mid palaces, lagoons and skies aflame?
Ah, to recall will then, like falling leaves,
Crown memory with the summer that it grieves.

A Roman Day

Below me, by the Pincian wall,
A Roman mother goes,
And wheels within a shaded pram
A lord of silken bows,
Attended by his slave, as once,
On a far summer's day,
Augustus Caesar, two years old,
Went to the park to play.

In the Ringstrasse, Vienna

Here in the Ringstrasse walking,
'Mid the scent of the summer limes,
I heard my young ghost talking
Of the lovelier, earlier times.

'Be quiet, be gone!' I protested,
'Enough of those vanished charms,
The Future's brightly attested
By the young in each other's arms.'

Empires fall, and the princes
Decay in a sunless slum;
Though Time's cold wisdom convinces,
Youth's folly is God's kingdom come.

Merano

So little to hoard through the long, long years,
To keep, to cherish, so fragile, so fleet,
So vain to recall, so futile the tears,
And yet at the sound of your voice, of your feet
On that mountain path, how my heart would leap!
And the valley's floor and the shining crown
Of the snowy heights, with their canyons deep,
Would flower again, where Merano town
Shakes down its music from steeple and tower.
Oh my love, oh my love, from that morning of gold,
Time hath not withered a single flower
Nor dimmed the image I deathlessly hold!

A poodle, descending

(For Mrs Aubrey Cartwright's Jet)

Black head, white teeth, clipped, curled, the beau complete,
As snowflakes fall, so lightly fall his feet.
If in the world of Dog a royal race is,
Here comes the Prince. Behold! whate'er his pace is,
The ceremonial, the gay, the antic,
Alike his charm drives all adorers frantic;
To get one look, one lick from our Prince Charming
Is to be happy—to be ignored, alarming.
So see us suppliant when, down the stairs,
Attired for social state, the Prince appears:
How arch his look, his captivating smile,
What rogueish eyes he'll roll, and with what guile
Advance you in his favour, but to turn
Tail upon you, and your fond service spurn,
Unless it be, with tact and manner meet,
Your offer takes a form the Prince can eat.
Fond of the boudoir, given to the bed,
A lover always, yet he keeps his head,
Reserved and cautious, for, in his opinion,
Only one lady's worth his heart's dominion;
On her his love he lavishes, avows
His worship of the lady of the House;
Let fickle fancy roam, false hearts forget,
No blackness can blackout the love of Jet.

A poodle, dancing

(For Lady Jekyll's Ben)

Timorously treading, the curled darling goes,
A harlequin dog, on delicate toes;
Elegant gentleman! Do you suppose
He's a Prince of the Blood with his Bourbon nose?
Beruffed, he dances, with royal disdain,
A pavan for a poodle, to music from Spain.

Six Phases

First, the small baby,
Two round eyes,
And no nose
Discernible yet, with crinkly toes;
And all day long he cries and cries.

Then the slim boy
Who will play,
Scorning girls,
Spending hours where the mill-race whirls,
Damming it up, watching it run away, away.

Soon the lank youth,
With his tie,
Plastered hair,
And the confident look in his eye,
Save when he dreams of a face so fair, so fair!

Next, the young man,
With brisk walk,
Strong hands,
And a longing to see strange lands,
And a passion to argue, and talk and talk.

Then the father
With a joke
For his boy
On his knee at bedtime—and soon to enjoy
Rest in the garden chair, and to smoke and smoke.

Last, the old fellow,
On his nose
A bright drop,
Never falling, and never appearing to stop,
And the old bent head that will doze and doze.

*Lightfoot Iphyclus

*'Over the spikes of the ripened corn he would run
and they not wilt.'*—HESIOD

Iphyclus within his bower
Woke at dawn, and from a rose
Shook the dewdrops for a shower,
Clad himself in petal clothes,
Pulled upon his twinkling feet
Moth-wing shoon, and blithely went
Running o'er the ripened wheat
So lightly not an ear was bent,
No furrow shadowed where he crossed.
Then, upon a butterfly
He lighted, and, on wings embossed,
Rode the smiling summer sky;
Now, a sparkling sea beneath
With jade-green paths, his fancy caught,
And, seizing on a falling leaf,
Adown the azure heaven was brought
To the bright, foam-marbled strand,
Where, harnessing a hippocampus,
Leaping dolphins on each hand,
He drove to lunch with old Melampus.

The Old Brown Hat

(*John Betjeman's*)

From Wantage way, half-Horace and half-Puck,
You came when Spring renewed the meads, and stood,
One foot upon my fender, fresh in luck
From an encounter in a Chiltern wood,

The wanton's kiss still glowing on your face,
The new-born ecstasy bright in your eyes,
And there recited, at a breathless pace,
The lines she gave you in that swift surprise.

Later, when you had gone, and wondering at
The spell that words have put on us long years,
I suddenly saw your old brown, battered hat,
Forgotten—and, somehow, came near to tears.

*The Closed Villino

I often think of you, dear Max,
Upon your terrace walking,
Rapallo's bay below you spread,
Our laughter and our talking.
How gay you were, blue reefer coat,
White flannels and white shoes,
Straw boater and—the dandy's note—
The white gardenia you would choose,
A buttonhole from the garden made
Along the terraced hillside where,
On flat-tiled roof, with balustrade,
You paced in the bright morning air.

Then in the noonday heat, beneath
The shade of an umbrella, we
Lunched, with a bottle deftly chosen—
What food, what talk, what gaiety!
Your china-blue, round, innocent eyes,
Your quiet voice, no warning gave
Of that stiletto tongue, that wise
Wit-laden comment, gay or grave.

There, from the little study blue,
That looked upon a bluer sea,
A curving bay and, glimmering far,
The Portofino promontory,
You saw the warm Italian day
Pass into the still, starry night,
The glittering lights around the bay,
The cypress black in the moon's light.

So day and month and year slipped by,
The long years gave you peace and fame,
The loving care of gentle hands.

Now you have gone, and never the same
That hillside where your villa stands;
The terrace hears no footsteps pass,
The booklined room a master lacks;
We'll laugh and dine no more, alas—
Farewell, incomparable Max!

*A Knight of Nottingham

In the town of Byron and Lawrence,
Of Kirke White and 'Festus' Bailey,
I took a tram to the Market Place
And worked in an office daily.

Oh, I was young and poor and eager,
An orphan of scarce sixteen,
But I walked in fields Elysian
Though none knew where I had been.

The office door was my Propylaea,
The tram stop my Acropolis,
And I was armed with shield and spear,
A hoplite bound for Salamis.

I used the office typewriter,
I used the Government's paper,
And went to court the great Eliza,
And showed slim legs in a caper.

Eight shillings a week I earned, and gave
Seven-and-six to my mother dear,
But with sixpence I went to Thessaly,
Or talked with the daughters of old King Lear.

In the town of the perplexed Sheriff
Who collided with Robin Hood,
I lived long days in Arcady,
A lad none understood.

Now I am old and passing rich
And have flirted a little with flighty Fame,
But I envy that boy with his heady dreams,
And a pen for a sword to make his name.

In the town of Booth and Barrie,
I now meet the ghost of a boy
With bright young eyes, who once kept watch
On the ramparts of windy Troy.

To my Mother
(E.M.R. 1855–1927)

I have not sung for you
One line of all the tribute I would pay,
But oh, if you knew
The things that crowd in my heart
At the thought of you,
Then might you say—
'To me belongs
The Song of Songs!'

The Wish

The fisher with a line
Catches his shining prey,
The hunter with a gun
Shoots down his bright-winged birds;
Would it were given to me,
Child of the mortal day,
To snare, in a noose of words,
One song Time cannot slay.

Notes

This selection of poems covers fifty years, 1910–60. Many of them are published for the first time. In 1912, aged twenty, I made my first appearance in print with *The Trent*, a poem which had won the Henry Kirke White Memorial Prize. There followed, between 1913 and 1918, five books of verse. In 1920 these were published in U.S.A. in one volume under the title of *Collected Poems*, to which John Masefield contributed a preface. This was my last book of verse. Since I sought to earn a living with my pen, I sent the Muse into exile and turned to more remunerative work in prose. But the master passion was always there, so I wrote my poems and put them away during the next forty years. From time to time I took them out to polish them, fashioning the words like the mosaic workers of the old Cosmati School, ever mindful of Chaucer's definition—'The lyfe so short, the craft so long to lerne, th'assay so hard, so sharp the conquering.'

Throughout this time I have attached myself to no school or fashion, following only the Miltonic dictum that poetry should be 'simple, sensuous and passionate'.

PAGE 14. *The Moon a lovely maiden is*

This poem, written in 1904, at the age of twelve, antedates the collection. Inspired by the gift of a telescope, I had begun a six-volume *History of the Stars*. The poem prefaced the first chapter, beyond which the work never progressed. I recited it to my father, announcing that I should die young in Italy, like Keats and Shelley. 'Precocious and indecent,' was his comment when I had recited the poem, but he gave me sixpence, remuneration prophetically small.

PAGE 20. *To John Masefield*

Written after visiting him at Boar's Hill, Oxford, in 1919. At the bottom of his garden I saw a young man in shorts wheeling two babies in a wheelbarrow. I

143

wondered who he was and Masefield explained. 'That's a young poet who's living with his wife and babies in our small cottage.' I thought he said his name was Robert Graves. Forty years later Graves confirmed the fact.

PAGE 21. *Springtime in Cookham Dean*

When a very young man, just arrived in London, I was fortunate in meeting Grant Richards who, with his remarkable flair, had been the early publisher of A. E. Housman, Bernard Shaw and John Galsworthy. In 1917 he published my *Twenty-Six Poems*, and the next year *Charing Cross and other Poems*, an act of courage. He was a handsome, debonair man and an exquisite host. He entertained me often at Bigfrith, Cookham Dean, where he kept an incomparable table. It was he who showed me the cherry trees, on that walk on which he had so often taken Housman, from Cookham Dean down through the orchards, when they were 'wearing white for Eastertide', to Cookham and the Thames. I dedicated this poem to him and his charming young wife.

PAGE 24. *Lines to a Dendronphobe*

Arriving one summer's day, in 1949, for lunch at Dropmore, Bucks, Lord Kemsley's country house, I found my hostess distressed by the cutting down of a noble tree that graced the horizon. The word 'dendronphobe' does not exist, but I think it should, for they do.

PAGE 25. *The Elm in Leaf*

A magnificent elm stood in the field of a property I owned at Fawley Green, Bucks. I often wondered who was my long-dead benefactor. It had grown until, from its branches, St George's Tower at Windsor Castle could be seen across the Thames valley.

PAGE 37. *Pilgrim Cottage Poems*

The poems in this group belong to the Pilgrim Cottage period, 1930–40. Most of them appeared in my three country books, *Gone Rustic*, *Gone Rambling*, *Gone Afield*.

PAGE 43. *Prayer for an old gardener*

With the purchase of Pilgrim Cottage I had inherited an ancient gardener who, at eighty, by devotion, had a stronger claim to cottage and garden than I.

PAGE 54. *The Village Blacksmith*

He was Mark Harman, aged eighty-five, who lived with his apple-cheeked wife, aged eighty-two, on my property, The Forge, Fawley Green, Bucks.

They had an old-world courtesy, and now lie together in the venerable churchyard, within the shadow of an ancient yew and the square tower where he was a bellringer.

The Garden Well

The well at my cottage was fifty-eight feet deep, with a windlass and bucket that stood under an apple tree. Alas, an architect ran the waste water into it. This weakened the seventeenth-century brickwork and the well collapsed. What, three hundred years ago, had probably cost a pound to build, would now cost two hundred to repair, so it was filled in.

In Memoriam

Nadja Malacrida, wife of the Marchese Pietro Malacrida, and niece of Lord Cowdray, was killed, a few minutes after leaving my cottage, where she had spent the summer of 1934, by the overturning of her sports car. Young, lovely, gifted, she created a *salon* in her London home, and was 'sung' by Humbert Wolfe, among others. She lies buried within sight of the cottage, under a memorial by Gilbert Ledward, R.A.

Louis Tissier

My secretary, a young Frenchman, beloved of many. He died at twenty-six after two years' heroic battle with consumption, following a chill caught in the French Alps during his military service. He had two passions—Pilgrim Cottage, and going to Woolworth's.

A Garden Revisited

> *Nessun maggior dolore* . . .—irrevocably true
> That sorrow of sorrows the Florentine knew.

Dante, *The Divine Comedy. Inferno. v.121*:

> *Nessun maggior dolore*
> *Che ricordarsi del tempo felice*
> *Nella miseria.*

'There is no greater sorrow than to recall a time of happiness in misery.'

A Man Arose

Written in March, 1941. After an introduction by Wendell Willkie, then Presidential candidate, I read this poem, on behalf of the British War Relief Society, New York, over the National Broadcasting Company's network in the United States and Canada. It was relayed to South America, Europe and India. I repeated the reading on behalf of Bundles For Britain. It was relayed four times. The N.B.C. presented Prime Minister Churchill with the recording. The poem was published, simultaneously, in the U.K. and the U.S.A. The royalties and copyright were given to the Royal Air Force Benevolent Fund. The manuscript is in the Library of Congress, Washington D.C.

PAGE 76. *Entering Mons*

With my fellow war-correspondents I entered Mons on the morning of November 11th, 1918, a few minutes before the Armistice. Later, on the reviewing stand outside the Hôtel de Ville, we saw the 7th Brigade of the 3rd Canadian Division march into the Grand Place. Promptly on the hour of eleven a bugle sounded the 'Cease Fire', and the Great World War came to an end. Headed by a pipers' band, the Canadian Black Watch marched in, to delirious cheering. There followed the playing by massed bands of *La Brabançonne* and the British *National Anthem*. It was at Mons that the British Army first made contact with the Germans, on August 23rd, 1914, and for three days, in a costly battle, 'the contemptible little army' held up the overwhelming German army. There the Black Watch had fought, and it was fitting that a contingent of the Canadian Black Watch should take part in the triumphant return to Mons.

PAGE 78. *Captain Albert Ball*, V.C., D.S.O., M.C.

At nineteen he was the famed flying ace of the Royal Flying Corps, in the First World War. Born at Nottingham, he was the very incarnation of the Elizabethan spirit, adventurous, chivalrous, modest. A much-sought-after enemy, he would not let the War Office keep him at home for propaganda purposes, but, in the flower of his fame, insisted on returning to the Front. The night after he had brought down his fortieth German, he wrote: 'Oh, won't it be nice when all this beastly killing is over, and we can enjoy ourselves and not hurt anyone! I hate this game, but it is the only thing one can do just now.' There was a mystery about his end; he disappeared fighting.

PAGE 79. *So Immortal a Flower*

The Crete campaign lasted from May 20th, 1941 to May 31st when the island was captured by the German Luftwaffe. It was a desperate, ill-starred adventure in which we lost fifteen thousand men. My novel of the Crete campaign, *So Immortal a Flower*, carries the same title.

PAGE 82. *Futility*

Written in 1917, and first published in *Today*. Its editor, Holbrook Jackson, wrote in a letter, March 23rd, 1922: 'Ralph Hodgson took tea with me last evening and, apropos of nothing, said: "The more I think of *Futility* the more I am convinced it is a great poem. When London is a desert some survivor will be chanting 'Who cares a damn who died at Salamis?' and, in the next war, that line will be quoted, not by the pacificists, but by the men who go out—ironically." This is about the third time or more he has spoken along these lines.' A generous salute from a veteran of the Muse.

PAGE 91. *The Golden Journey from Samarkand*

In 1913 James Elroy Flecker published *The Golden Journey to Samarkand*, which at once established his fame. He was then dying of consumption in Switzerland. In my youthful discovery of this book I wrote to him. He replied: 'Do write again. It is jolly to be admired in a jolly way.' He died eighteen months later, aged thirty. In this poem I have adopted the style and subject of his poem, reversing the journey his pilgrims made; 'variations on a theme'.

PAGE 98. *To Shelley, after seeing Ozymandias*

Shelley's famous sonnet runs:

> I met a traveller from an antique land
> Who said: Two vast and trunkless legs of stone
> Stand in the desert. . . .
> My name is Ozymandias, king of kings:
> Look on my works, ye Mighty, and despair.

In 1955, at Thebes, I looked on his trunkless legs. He wrote over the portal of his library, in Hundred-gated Thebes, an inscription, of which only the Greek translation has survived—Ψυχης ιατρειον, which may be translated 'The Soul's Dispensary.' Diodorus Siculus called the Ramesseum (of Rameses II) the tomb of Ozymandias.

PAGE 103. *Nicoletta*

Nicoletta Panni, granddaughter of the famed Giuseppe di Luca. A young Italian, she has sung in most of the capitals of Europe. One day in her Roman home, before departing for a season of Italian opera in London, she sang for us some of her arias. I wrote these lines in her album, the Italian version running:

> Quando Nicoletta canta
> Io sento cento cose—
> Uccelli nel bosco,
> Canarini in gabbia,
> Ed impetuosi venti di Marzo
> Lungo la spiaggia di un mare tempestoso.

Quando Nicoletta canta
Ricordo mille cose—
Il sogno che un giovane ragazzo
Conobbe in Primavere incantate,
E non dimenticate, il dolore, la gioia,
Che riemperono tanti anni,
Ritornano ora
Con amore velato da lagrime—
Quando Nicoletta canta.

PAGE 109. *Lines for the unveiling of Haydn's portrait by Fuseli*

Read one evening at Mrs Murray Crane's, Fifth Avenue, New York, to celebrate her acquisition of the portrait made by Fuseli during Haydn's visit to London in 1794. A quartet played one of Haydn's compositions at the unveiling.

PAGE 110. *Lines Completed*

How odd of God . . . The first four lines are by W. N. Ewer (1885–).
Twinkle, twinkle, little star . . . The lines are by Jane Taylor (1783–1827).
O what a tangled web . . . Sir Walter Scott 1771–1832.

PAGE 113. *The Priest of Sant' Ambrogio*

On July 8th, 1922, armed with a letter of introduction, I lunched for the first time with Max Beerbohm, at the Villino Chiaro, near Rapallo. To make sure that I should not arrive late on this momentous occasion, I went out the previous evening to reconnoitre the position of his villa, and got lost, in the moonlight, on the mountainside. Thirty years later, again visiting Max, I went back to that little church where I had encountered the priest, to find mourners coming out from his memorial service.

PAGE 119. *Strip Poker. Harvard, 1920*

In March, 1920, I was the guest of a young American at Harvard University. Prohibition had been introduced on January 1st of that year, and resulted in an orgy of private drinking, bootlegging and the menace of death from home-made alcoholic concoctions. The Act defeated its intention, and later was re-pealed. Our run, towards midnight, took us over the frozen snow, along the bank, and on to the bridge over the River Charles, at Cambridge, where Longfellow had stood, musing, as in his famous poem:

> I stood on the bridge at midnight,
> As the clocks were striking the hour.

Gondola, signore? . . . Gùn-dohla, not the English pronunciation, Gon-dòh-la. But I have kept the English pronunciation (Shakespeare's) Des-de-mona, and not the Italian, Des-dèmona. *Palazzo Vendramin*: Built in 1481 by Pietro Lombardo for the noble Loredan family. The palace cost 200,000 ducats. In 1581 it was sold to the Duke of Brunswick for 50,000 ducats. In 1583 it was bought by the Duke of Mantua for 91,000 ducats. A legal dispute resulted in an auction, when it fell to Vettor Calergi for 30,000 ducats. In 1608 it passed by marriage to Vicenzo Grimani. His sons committed a murder there in 1658, and by order of the Signory the left wing was demolished, but rebuilt in 1690. By marriage it then passed to Nicolò Vendramin. In 1884 it was sold to the Duchesse de Berri, and later was inherited by the Comte de Chambord. Richard Wagner died there on February 13th, 1883. It was famous for some jasper columns, fine chimney-pieces in ebony and ivory, and for statues of Adam and Eve, removed from the mausoleum of Doge Andrea Vendramin in SS. Giovanni and Paolo, and now in the Metropolitan Museum, New York. I used to visit a Mrs Davey there, who lived on the *piano nobile*, and Karl Vollmöller, the author of *The Miracle*, who lived on the top floor.

Byron first saw Teresa Guiccioli in 1819, at a *conversazione* at Countess Benzoni's palace in Venice. Aged thirty-one, he was then living in the Palazzo Mocenigo on the Grand Canal. At sixteen, Teresa was the wife of the elderly Count Guiccioli. The liaison that began then lasted until 1823, when Byron went to Greece, and to his death at Missolonghi.

At one time in Venice, I lived in the Campo Fenice. The back of my lodging opened on to a small canal, and an alley leading to the large Campo S. Angelo. In this Square there is a house, marked with a plaque, in which Domenico Cimarosa lived and died. I passed it often in daylight and moonlight, with its pointed Gothic-Venetian windows. In his day it was the *Locanda delle Tre Stelle*—The Three Stars Inn. Cimarosa was born in Naples in 1749, went to Rome at twenty-four, and won notice with a humorous opera, *The Italian in London*. In turn, he lived in Rome, Venice, Florence, St Petersburg, where he was Court Musician, and in Vienna, where he produced his masterpiece, *Il Matrimonio Segreto*. A republican, on the return to Naples of the Bourbons, he was condemned to death, pardoned by Ferdinand, exiled, and went to Venice, where he died January 11th, 1801.

Giardino Eden, Venice

The Garden of Eden, on the Giudecca at Venice, took its name from the fact that it was the summer home of the Eden family in the Eighteen Nineties. It was acquired later by Aspasia, Princess Alexander of Greece, widow of King Alexander of Greece, and mother of ex-Queen Alexandra of Jugoslavia. She has made it a centre of hospitality to many visitors to Venice. It is located behind the church of the Redentore. The long, low-walled garden, with its vines and cypresses, commands a superb view of the Venetian lagoons and the Euganean Hills.

PAGE 136. *Lightfoot Iphyclus*

The poem was suggested by Hesiod's epigram.

I have assumed that his Iphyclus was the lightfooted athlete, later King of Phylace. His connection with Melampus was singular. The latter, licked by serpents in his sleep, became a seer, philosopher and physician, capable of translating the speech of birds. But he allowed his brother to persuade him to steal the famous bulls of Iphyclus. Caught in the act, he was shut up in a chest, but when the lid was raised he was alive, having commanded the bees to feed him with honey through the keyhole. Iphyclus, impressed, freed him, and, childless, was taught by him how to become a father. Melampus had other gifts. He restored to sanity the women of Argos, smitten by madness, for which King Anaxagoras gave him part of his kingdom. Melampus and his posterity reigned for six generations. According to Herodotus, he taught the Greeks the name of Dionysos, and introduced the phallic procession in honour of the god. After death he received divine honours, and six temples were raised to his memory. No wonder that Iphyclus went to lunch with the old gentleman.

PAGE 138. *The Closed Villino*

The Villino Chiaro, near Rapallo, was the home of Sir Max Beerbohm, the cartoonist and essayist, from 1919 until his death there in 1956. His eightieth year witnessed a great celebration among his friends and admirers all over the world.

PAGE 140. *A Knight of Nottingham*

Byron, when a boy of ten, lived in St James's Street, Nottingham. *D. H. Lawrence* (1885–1930) went to the University College there. *Henry Kirke White* (1785–1806) was taken up by Southey as the result of a book of poems published when he was eighteen. He was mentioned by Byron in his verses. A butcher's son, he obtained a Sizarship at St John's College, Cambridge, where he died of excessive study. I spent my youth in an office in a maze of butchers' shops, known as The Shambles, under the old Exchange, now pulled down. I looked across a dark alley at the butcher's shop where Kirke White was born. It bore a memorial plaque, warning me of the early deaths of poets. Kirke White must have been a melancholy youth for he wrote:

> The worm it doth riot on heavenly diet
> When Death hath deflowered the eye.

But he also wrote the verses from which the hymn *Onward, Christian Soldiers* was derived. *Festus Bailey* (1816–1902): Born in Nottingham. In 1840 he published his poem, *Festus*. On the strength of this he lived, famous, in all the encyclopaedias, and with a Civil List pension, for the next sixty-two years, and never again wrote anything worth reading. *General William Booth* (1829–1912): Born in Nottingham, he was the founder of The Salvation Army. When he was seventy-nine I saw him, like an Old Testament prophet, standing in a carriage, acclaimed by the crowd, as he rode to the Exchange to receive the Freedom of the City. *Sir James Barrie* (1860–1937): He began his career, after leaving Edinburgh University, as the leader-writer and editor of *The Nottingham Journal*, in February, 1883. Almost forty years later, when I succeeded to the editorship, he told me that his salary had been three pounds, three shillings a week.